THE CLASSIC
MG

THE CLASSIC
MG

RICHARD ASPDEN

53 MG TD

HAMLYN

LONDON · NEW YORK · SYDNEY · TORONTO

A Bison Book

This paperback edition published by
The Hamlyn Publishing Group Limited
London   New York   Sydney   Toronto
Astronaut House, Feltham
Middlesex, England

Produced by Bison Books Corp.
17 Sherwood Place,
Greenwich, Ct 06830
USA

ISBN 0 600 50021 7

Printed in Hong Kong

Page 2 and 3: A classic MG sportscar, the 1953 TD.
Below: A much-modified 1935 P-type 'Boogazoo Special'

Contents

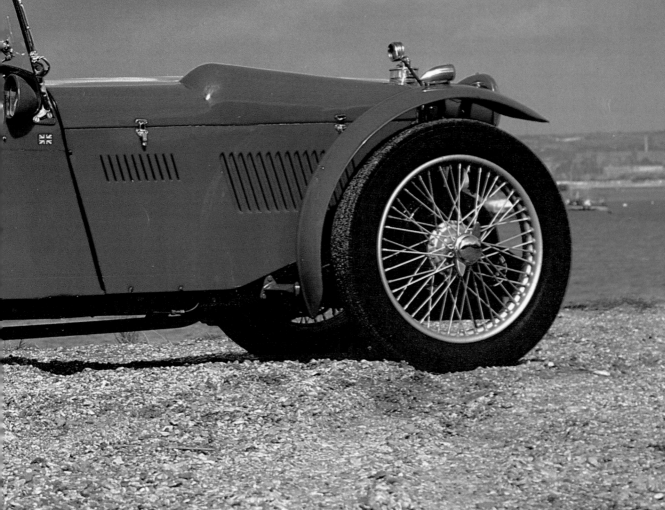

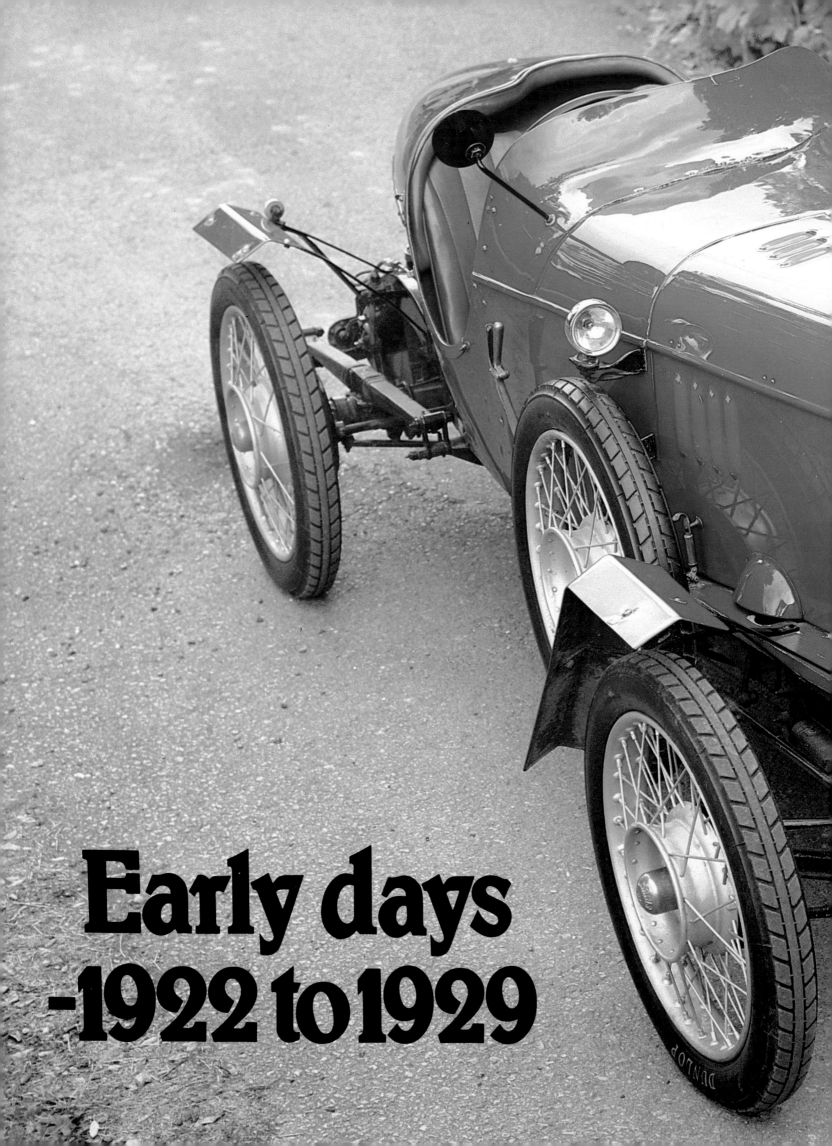

Early days -1922 to 1929

Part of the enormous collection at the BL Heritage Museum, this is probably their most envied item, going back to 1929 – the very first MG ever produced.

It is somehow fitting that the final draft of this book was begun the very week chosen by British Leyland to announce the rebirth of MG. The last few years have not been happy ones for the worldwide band of enthusiasts who for almost 60 years have enjoyed and loved the sportscars from the small factory in Abingdon. Now it seems the unhappy period of stagnation and confusion is over and we can again look forward to a new generation of sporting automobiles bearing the famous octagon.

Like so many of the better things in this world, the marque MG was the brainchild of one man whose vision and determination aided by the loyalty and dedication of a small, highly skilled team, brought a dream to reality.

Cecil Kimber was born in the London suburb of Dulwich on 12 April 1888, the family moving to the North of England some eight years later where his father, Francis Henry Kimber, joined his brother in running a printing ink manufacturing company. Growing up, the young Cecil seems to have shown little interest in this rather prosaic business, his talents lying more in the direction of mechanical engineering, an interest leading inevitably to motorcycling. It was entirely typical of his approach to the subject that much of his time was spent stripping and rebuilding his machines in apparently successful attempts to improve performance and reliability.

A serious accident while riding a borrowed Rex almost caused the loss of his right leg. After what must have been a painful period involving a number of operations the damaged limb at last began to heal, though it was to leave him with a leg shortened by two inches, resulting in a permanent limp. A more positive aspect of this misfortune was the award of a useful sum, reputedly in the region of £700 (then $3500) in compensation. A further unlooked for advantage of this disability was that it would exempt him from military service in the approaching World War, leaving him to pursue his engineering talents. With part of his award he bought his first car, a 12hp Singer. This served him faithfully over a large mileage, mostly covered as a representative for his father's firm. The business was failing however, and after a bitter quarrel concerning Cecil's refusal to put some of his own money into the ailing concern, father and son went their separate ways, the elder Kimber refusing ever again to speak to his son. Though in later years Cecil made many attempts to bridge the rift between them, his father would have nothing to do with him, maintaining his stony silence to the end.

Kimber had good reason for not wishing to risk the remainder of his small capital. He had met and wished to marry a Manchester girl, Irene Hunt, who supported him in his conviction that his future lay in the motor industry. In 1915, aged 26, he took his first job in this field, joining Sheffield – Simplex, a Yorkshire firm founded by the Earl Fitzwilliam for the manufacture of high grade luxury cars. Later that year he and Irene, or Renee, as she was known, were married.

The next few years were spent with various firms within the industry until 1921 when he accepted the position that was to mark the turning point of his career. He became Sales Manager of Morris Garages, the leading automobile retail outlet in the city of Oxford.

In character Kimber was deeply conservative with a strong sense of his own capabilities, tending to become prickly whenever these were questioned or doubted. Essentially a serious minded, creative personality his sense of humor was nevertheless surprisingly schoolboyish. Yet despite a sometimes difficult temperament he always possessed that gift peculiar to men of deep conviction of retaining the dedicated

Above: In charge of the Morris Garages at Oxford, Cecil Kimber was the man who created the very first MG and went on to forge the new marque into a legend on road and track.

Right: This was his creation, based on the new (in 1929) Morris Minor engine and a fabric body which cost £6 10s.

loyalty of his workforce. Above all perhaps, he possessed the driving force and imagination to enable him to extract maximum potential from ground in which the seeds of success were far from obvious. But if he was perhaps not always the easiest of men to get along with, all those who knew him well speak of his great personal charm, a quality evidently removing the sting from his more irascible moments.

Much has been written of his organizing ability but little of the artistic side of his complex character. That he was a creative engineer is obvious but the creative aspect of his nature extended to include an exceptional eye for line and form, some of his designs for coachwork on MG chassis being of outstanding merit judged by any standard.

The man for whom he was now working was altogether different. William Richard (Billy) Morris was a selfmade motor industry tycoon who had started, like many others of his kind in Europe and the US by repairing and selling bicycles. From these beginnings he had branched out into the motorcycle trade, selling the rights of this highly successful operation to his partner Edward Armstead in 1908. In 1911 he opened newly converted premises in Oxford's Longwall Street as an automobile showroom, acquiring further premises in the same street as the business expanded over the next two years. These became Morris Garages Ltd.

But his ambitions lay beyond merely selling automobiles. Morris wanted to join the ranks of the car makers and this era saw the construction of a large new factory in the Oxford suburb of Cowley. His first car, the 10hp Oxford was well received in the immediate pre-World War period, becoming, alongside the later Cowley, the company's staple product until the mid 1920s. Initially known as WRM Motors Ltd, this was changed in 1919 to Morris Motors Ltd. So the early 1920s saw William Morris controlling two expanding organizations, one manufacturing automobiles, the other, under the direction of his friend Edward Armstead, a successful new car retail outlet handling, besides Morris cars, such makes as Hupmobile, Wolseley, Standard, Singer, Arrol-Johnston, Belsize and Humber. Nothing exciting, just stolid cars designed to appeal to the solid middle classes of England's South Midlands.

As an engineer Morris was sound rather than innovative and shrewd rather than adventurous as a motor industry baron. Despite having been a successful competitor in his cycling and motorcycling days by the time Kimber had joined his organization he was deeply opposed to factory participation in competition on the grounds that it was both costly and unnecessary.

For reasons unclear to this day Armstead suddenly resigned as General Manager, tragically committing suicide a few weeks later. Under these somber circumstances Kimber was promoted to General Manager. With this new hand on the helm the company not only continued to flourish but to gradually change its course as Kimber set about realizing his ambitions.

To this end he started designing and building specialist, or custom bodies for the Morris Cowley. The most distinctive aspect of this somewhat homely vehicle was its handsomely

Left: Small, lightweight and amazingly inexpensive, the very first MG began a long tradition of fast sportscars which anyone could afford but which had power and handling well beyond their rather lowly price bracket.

Right: The 1929 split-screen roadster.

rounded radiator, this giving rise to the affectionate 'Bull-nose' nickname by which both the Cowley and its larger stablemate the 'Oxford' were known. Current until 1927 these prosaic family automobiles were the stock from which MG was to emerge as a make in its own right.

Here we reach the vexed question; which was the first MG? This is a subject on which lifetime enthusiasts for the marque have argued. It is impossible to pinpoint any particular car as being the seminal MG. The fact is that the marque was gradually evolved over a period of seven or eight years, though its existence as a separate entity from the parent concern, Morris Garages Ltd was not officially recognized until 21 July 1930 when it was registered as the MG Car Company Ltd. The one thing of which we can be certain is that the special trials car constructed between 1924/1925 and known for years as 'Old Number One' is not the first true MG!

With hindsight it is evident that Kimber's ambitions from the start of his employment by Morris Garages leant towards the creation of a new make embodying his ideas. His first step in this direction was to design an alternative body for the Cowley. This was in effect a close coupled tourer, its chief advantage over the standard two-seat plus dicky seat version being that all four occupants were protected by the top when it rained, though otherwise it's doubtful if rear passengers traveled in any more comfort, the seating area to the rear being decidedly cramped. The Chummy, as it was called was an immediate success, over 200 being sold through 1922/23. Then it suddenly became obsolete upon the introduction by Morris Motors of an almost identical model, the Cowley Occasional Four for rather less money. Kimber's own personal Chummy gave him a modest competition success when, after slight tuning he and his co-driver qualified for one of 53 gold medals awarded in the London to Lands End trial.

Next, a mildly modified Cowley chassis was fitted with a rather pretty two-seat sporting body built under Kimber's direction by Charles Raworth, a local coachbuilding concern. With their elegantly curved fenders and raked windshields supported on either side by triangular glass frames these were distinctly sporting cars. The overall effect was heightened by a pair of marine type ventilators placed on top of the firewall. These features were to become an MG hallmark, appearing on all subsequent MGs until 1929. Some consider the 'Raworth' to be the first true MG, for though the radiator badge clearly stated it to be a Morris, there appeared in 1924 an advertisement where for the first time the stylized letters MG were used within the octagon motif, the car being described as 'The MG Super Sports Morris.' Mild modifying of the 1548cc four-cylinder L head Hotchkiss engine enabled it to approach 60mph, but despite claims that the price was 'modest' at £350 ($1750) it evidently wasn't modest enough and only six were sold. This period also saw Kimber designing alternative coachwork for the larger 14.9hp Morris Oxford chassis. These included a vee front saloon, tourer, and even a landaulette, a formal style whose configuration was virtually that of a six-cylinder light saloon in which the rear quarter had an openable top. None of these achieved any great success but it is worth noting that they were all advertised as MGs, though to Kimber's intense irritation, on the rare occasions that the Press mentioned them, they were invariably referred to as 'special bodied Morrises.' Though this was a perfectly fair description, Kimber's annoyance coupled with his efforts to imbue the cars with their own identity is clear indication of the direction of his ambitions.

During this year (1924) Kimber had been approached by a well known trials driver, Billy Cooper, who wanted an improved version of the now discontinued Morris Cowley Sports, of which he had used three with considerable success.

Kimber based his car on a special bodied 14/28 Morris Oxford owned by one of his salesmen, incorporating in its design a number of improvements to the body and chassis. These consisted of lowering the chassis to obtain better handling and to improve it as a base for sporting coachwork. Alterations were fairly simple, consisting of flattening the springs and raking the steering column. This in conjunction with a higher mounted steering box and longer drop arm gave improved steering control. The handsome four-seat tourer coachwork was finished in polished aluminum with blue fenders and valances. A further touch of elegance was supplied by the polished aluminum Ace disks covering the artillery wheels. Cooper was delighted with it, and the car was frequently parked near the starting line at Brooklands race track where Cooper assisted the famous 'Ebby' Ebblewhite in his duties as official starter and timekeeper. This was useful publicity for the car attracted much favorable comment.

In September 1924 the Morris range underwent considerable improvement; all Oxford chassis were lengthened and fitted with four wheel braking systems, while that of the tourer was further lengthened by six inches to nine feet. This was to form the basis of one of the most beautiful cars of the Vintage era. Having altered the chassis in much the same way as the Cooper car, Kimber subtly redrew the coachwork to produce a design of truly outstanding appearance. The center panels beneath the waistline were left in polished aluminum, as were the wheel disks, but the area of bodywork above the waistline, valances and fenders were painted, usually in a rich claret or smoke blue. The color of the paint was echoed in the leather upholstery. The impressive row of hood louvers was repeated further down the body along the firewall, while cast aluminum tread plates bearing the octagon motif to the rear of the running boards contributed to the overall air of quality. The by now

familiar sharply raked windshield with its triangular side panes and marine ventilators also featured to good effect, and the overall result gave an impression both of grace and strength. Examining one of these cars today it becomes evident that Kimber's treatment of mass and form, together with his imaginative use of color in conjunction with bare aluminum was masterly. The proportions are faultless and not a single jarring line disturbs the overall symetry.

Mechanical changes were limited to mild tuning of the side valve four and a higher back axle ratio. At this time Kimber quietly dropped any reference to Morris in advertising literature, simply calling the cars MG Super Sports. Selling at £375 ($1875), around 400 were built over the following two years along with several variants including a rather peculiar looking pointed tail 'Salonette.' Later versions of the tourer were fitted with bolt on wire wheels in place of the disk covered artillery type whereas those of the Salonette were of the steel disk variety wearing balloon tires.

Performance was commendable for a by no means lightweight touring car powered by a modest 1800cc 'cooking' engine. 'The Autocar' recorded a top speed of 65mph and reached 50mph from standstill in 24 seconds, figures not equalled by many bigger-engined, more expensive cars of the period.

And what of 'Old Number One?' This was a one-off special on which work had initially begun in 1924, built up from a combination of various standard and modified Morris parts. The engine used was an overhead valve version of the 11.9hp Hotchkiss engine used in the little-known Gilchrist car. Here it should be noted that with the exception of the OHV head this was identical to the Hotchkiss unit standard in the Cowley. First registered in March 1925, the car was finished in the dark grey used by MG for their prototypes and entered in the London to Lands End Trial in which it qualified for a gold medal, Kimber sharing the driving with a friend, Wilfred Matthews. Despite its excellent performance and handling nothing further was done with it by the Company. William Morris probably declined to support any further development of such an overtly sporting machine and the car was sold to a friend of Kimber's. It returned to the factory some years later only to become the subject of improbable legend at the hands of the publicity department during the Nuffield era. In the meantime the increasing demand for MGs dictated an urgent need for further premises which were secured in a section of Morris Motors Radiators Branch.

The much-loved Bullnose MGs were followed in late 1926 by a heavier, far less handsome flat radiatored model which, at first, retained the 14/28 Super Sports designation becoming the 14/40 Mark IV a year later. This step had been forced upon the Company by the redesign of the Morris range following a trip by W R Morris to the USA for the purpose of studying the latest production techniques. It was true that the Cowley and Oxford were rapidly becoming outdated but it was unfortunate for MG that the modernization of the cars on which they were based meant that they had to work with a new chassis which was both heavier and less amenable to the fitting of attractive coachwork. Thus the latest MG production was not only inferior in performance, its stiff, gawky lines made it the ugly duckling to its predecessor's swan.

Above: The 'Old Number One' racing special and (below) the production models. In 1929 the Mk 1 18/80 went from Oxford to Carbodies at Coventry where the bare chassis/engine was clothed. Some were given the Carlton touring body.

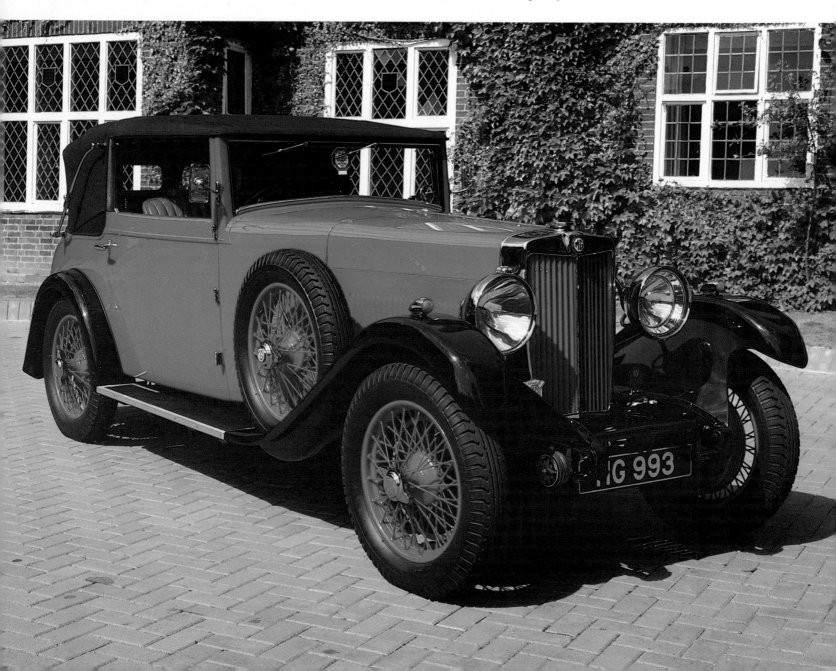

In 1927 two steps were taken towards making MG a make in its own right. Increased production to cope with demand indicated a dire need for proper factory premises, and Kimber persuaded Morris to provide the funds for a new factory in Edmund Road, Oxford. Later that year the marque's identity was confirmed when the cars appeared bearing the octagon badge on their radiators for the first time. This is being used today on BL's Maestros and Metros.

October 30 1927 saw the small company's first racing victory, at Buenos Aires of all places, when Alberto Cires comfortably beat seven other finishers to the checkered flag after an hour long sportscar race, his 14/40 averaging a spanking 62mph.

With a new fully equipped modern factory at his disposal Kimber was able to set about countering the 'rebodied Morris' taunt that was such anathema to him. Although it was true that engines and chassis were still of stock Morris origin, the chassis especially underwent considerable modification while engines were stripped down, cleaned and reassembled with meticulous care. In the interests of reliability tuning was restricted to enlarging and polishing the ports, the fitting of stronger valve springs and an improved magneto.

Kimber's obsession with marque identity reached something approaching absurd heights in 1928 when the 14/40 reappeared bedecked with octagons. On the instrument panel the round Smiths instruments had been replaced by octagonal ones, the accelerator bore an octagon motif, while yet another was cast into the aluminum toe board. Further octagons appeared on the wheel hubs and rear luggage locker and even the firewall ventilators had assumed an octagonal shape. Fortunately this craze for the octagonal stopped short of the steering wheel! By the time production finished in 1929 around 900 of these sturdy cars had been built.

But in the meantime something exciting had been brewing. On the MG stand at the 1928 London Motor Show the faithful 14/40 was eclipsed by two entirely new MGs. The MG Sports Six boasted a six-cylinder 2468cc single overhead camshaft engine featuring pressure fed lubrication, twin carburetors and shell bearings. The whole unit was a sturdily constructed affair with more than adequate reserves of strength. This splendid power unit was derived from the large Wolseley engine inherited by Morris Motors after purchasing the old established Wolseley concern in 1927. Wolseley had had considerable experience with overhead cam engines as a result of their wartime contract to build the famous Hispano-Suiza aircraft engine under licence.

The chassis of the 18/80 Sports Six, to give it its full title, was entirely new, owing nothing to any Morris. Designed by Kimber it was a sturdy structure of generally orthodox design incorporating semi-elliptic springing all round controlled by Hartford friction type dampers. Brakes were modified Morris and among the least satisfactory aspects of the car. Typical of the care that had gone into the design were the beautifully cast MG motifs each side of the aluminum firewall bulkhead brackets. An attractive if unnecessary detail perhaps, because once the body was fitted they were hidden from view.

The 18/80 was fast for its day, with a top speed of 78mph matched with a 10 to 50mph time of 16 seconds. These figures were recorded by a handsomely proportioned four door saloon and beat such quality competition as the Three Liter Lagonda and Alvis Silver Eagle. Though aimed at a richer clientel than previous MGs the 18/80 represented excellent value for money at prices ranging from £480 ($2400) for a two-seat sports to £555 ($2775) for the four-door saloon, the bare chassis costing £420 ($2100).

Excellent as it was however, the 18/80 was overshadowed by its companion on the stand. The crowd clustered thickest around a spindly-wheeled two-seat roadster, with cycle fenders, a boat tail and a raked Vee screen which emphasized a distinctly jaunty air. The MG Midget had arrived. Both the Midget's and the 18/80's identity was proudly proclaimed by a handsome new radiator design which was to endure almost unchanged on succeeding MGs for the next 27 years. Like that of the bigger car its engine was part of the Wolseley inheritance; one that was to prove of vital significance to Morris.

The arrival in 1922 of the Austin 'Seven' had created a new market of great potential. Whereas previously the marginal motorist had had to be content with a motorcycle and sidecar, or worse, one of the rash of poorly-engineered, unreliable cyclecars he could now buy a proper car for almost the same money.

The Seven's huge success inevitably attracted imitators, but few offered serious competition apart from the more upmarket Clyno. Though almost forgotten today Clyno had enjoyed a meteoric rise from nowhere to become one of Britain's major car makers in the mid to late 1920s, leaving Morris desperately needing something with which to enter the lucrative baby car market. The brilliant little Wolseley-designed 847cc single overhead cam four-cylinder engine provided the ideal base for just that. Installed in a lightweight prototype chassis, one of these units produced such startling performance that Morris engineers decided it needed detuning before being offered to the public in their forthcoming baby car. The original Morris Minor was launched late in 1928, and it was on this that the 'M' Type MG Midget was based.

The Minor engine and chassis remained practically unaltered, and the detuned unit's modest 20bhp gave the lightweight roadster a top speed of over 60mph with usefully brisk acceleration. But most attractive of all was the price of £175 ($875), only £50 ($250) more than the Minor. Over the next 12 months power was upped to a rousing 27bhp at 4500rpm and the Minor braking system redesigned. Both these improvements were the work of Reg Jackson, an engineer whose name was to figure prominently in forthcoming developments.

At the start of 1929 an 18/80 driven by Sir Francis Samuelson in the Monte Carlo Rally, won awards in the coachwork section and for making third best performance of the day in the Mont des Mules hillclimb. At Easter the by now familiar MG contingent acquitted themselves well in the London to Lands End Trial, while later in the year June saw the first invasion of Brooklands by the Midget in which a team driven by the Earl of March, H D Parker and Leslie Callingham scored three gold medals, a success repeated later in the year by a similar team.

The production of the Midget was well under way and MG were again outgrowing their premises; so the move was made to another factory in the small Berkshire town of Abingdon, where they were to remain for the next half century. Looking back on their efforts at the end of 1929 the men of MG had good reason to feel optimistic about the future. The company was now a marque in its own right, production had almost trebled and success in competition pointed the way to promising development in this direction. All these factors combined to infuse the small company with a spirit of dynamic energy that was to produce startling results over the next five years.

From the crucible of competition -1930 to 1935

The 'Cream Crackers' were one of three teams set up under the 1935 deal between Lord Nuffield and Leonard Lord. The others were The Musketeers and, in Scotland, the Blue Bustards. This is a PB in Cream Crackers colors. The inset picture shows another racing PB.

Late in 1929 the 18/80 was augmented by the 18/80 Mark II, though the original model remained in production as the Mark I. On the Mark II the already sturdy chassis was strengthened, the track increased to 52 inches, and a four-speed transmission featured for the first time on an MG. A New Dewandre servo operated system employed 14-inch drums, and the Mark I's 12-inch drums likewise were given the benefit of servo assistance. Unfortunately the extra weight imposed by these improvements led to a decrease in performance and a substantial increase in price; the two seat Mark II cost £625 ($3125) while the four door saloon was nudging the top end of the middle class market at £799 ($3495).

The Mark II provided the basis for the first competition MG, the 18/100 Mark III, sometimes known as Tiger, or Tigress. Extensive modification of the 2.5-liter unit included a more fiercely profiled camshaft, twin plug cross-flow head, new pistons and crank and dry sump lubrication, raising bhp from 60 to 83. This impressive machinery was installed in a modified Mark II chassis and fitted with a handsome four-seat lightweight tourer body. The lightweight effect was somewhat spoiled by the addition of deep, heavily louvered full length side valances giving the car a massive appearance.

The first Mark III, resplendant in brown and cream MG racing livery was due to make its debut in the Brooklands Double Twelve race on the second weekend in May 1930, driven by Leslie Callingham and H D Parker. This was one of the major events in the British calendar. Twenty four hours of racing took place over two days so that the stockbroking inhabitants of nearby Weybridge could sleep undisturbed by the thunder of racing cars.

It was an inauspicious occasion. The car was hopelessly overweight and the engine proved unable to withstand sustained high revs, running its bearings after a couple of hours. Further experiment demonstrated the engine's unsuitability for this kind of work and the model was dropped after only five had been constructed. It was also too expensive, retailing at £895 ($4775). Surplus Mark III bodies were mounted on Mark I chassis to produce the rather charming Mark I Speed Model, which with a genuine 80mph represented excellent value at only £525 ($2625). Between late 1928 and mid 1931 some 500 Mark Is were sold, just over double the total

Above: A C-type Midget racer.
Right: the M-type Midget racer,
the first of a long line of historic
race cars.

Left and below: The 1271 cc Type
F from 1932.

production of the Mark II, which lingered on well into 1933.

The big MG's disappointing performance in the Double Twelve was, however, offset by the fine demonstration of high speed reliability displayed by a team of Midgets in that event. Headed by Cecil Randall and co-driver F M Montgomery the factory-prepared team of five cars won the Team Prize, Randall coming in 14th after averaging 60.23mph over the 24 hours. This performance was all the more impressive because the cars were virtually standard apart from cutaway doors, the regulation Brooklands mufflers and large, clumsy looking gauze screens which cannot have helped the aerodynamics. These cars benefitted from H N Charles' improved valve timing which produced an increase from 20 to 27bhp which was also passed on to production versions.

This race was noteworthy in that it was the first time the Midget had been pitted against the side valve Austin Seven racing cars, which, with eight years development behind them, had been undisputed leaders in the 750cc class for a long time. Two Sevens finished ahead of the leading MG, so in this first bout honors were just about even. Later that year an Austin was to win the prestigious Brooklands 500 Mile race outright at an astonishing 83.4mph average.

An ever-growing band of private owners raced their Midgets at venues in countries as diverse as Czechoslovakia, South Africa, and Singapore. Meanwhile Kimber and Charles set to work on its successor. This was based on an experimental frame fabricated from mild steel tubing. For maximum rigidity the engine was carried in two tubular supports, one passing across the frame beneath the bell housing, the other extending forward from the front of the

engine to include the radiator mounting. This ensured that even when the chassis was subject to flexing the radiator remained rigidly in position. A further aspect of this frame was that aft the curvature of the front dumb irons it swept down beneath the rear axle thus making possible a sports car of really low build. Passing the springs through phosphor bronze trunnions instead of shackling them provided extra lateral rigidity. The wheelbase was 81 inches, an increase of 6 inches over the old Minor frame. This prototype chassis, christened EX 120, was not only to form the basic frame upon which all succeeding Midgets would be based until the arrival, almost two decades later, of the TD, it was also to make history in its own right.

Captain George Eyston and Ernest Eldridge were two of the leading figures in the record breaking field. They had been searching for a suitable car with which to attack the Class H (750cc) Hour record, then held by Austin. Examination of EX 120 convinced them that, fitted with a specially tuned M Type engine reduced to 750cc, it was their answer. Work proceeded apace in a top secret workshop in a corner of the factory. Reg Jackson and the scientific Eldridge between them converted what was essentially a small family car unit into a fully fledged record breaking engine. They reduced the bore and stroke to 81mm × 54mm (743cc) which was necessary to bring the engine within the 750cc limit. The operation consisted chiefly of strengthening the bottom end and extensively altering the valve gear, particular attention being paid to fine balancing. Wearing a vaguely streamlined body in which the basic form of the M Type was just discernible EX 120 was taken to Montlhéry, near Paris, where on 30 December 1930 Eyston averaged

Above left: Front view of the K1 from 1933 and, above right, the view that most other drivers saw most often – the back end.

Right: Engine detail of the K1 and, below, the business end of the engine from the driver's viewpoint.

87.3mph for 100 kilometers before a valve broke. The 'Hour' was still out of their grasp, but even so, several of Austin's records had already fallen to MG.

Malcolm Campbell was shortly due to attempt 100mph in a specially built Austin, but Kimber ordained that this milestone record must be captured by MG. Experiments with a Powerplus supercharger gave promising results, so early 1931 saw EX 120 once again at Montlhéry where, on the evening of Friday 26 February, with the aid of a streamlined front cowl fashioned on the spot from an old oil drum, Eyston achieved his goal taking four records at speeds up to 103.13mph. This was an amazing speed for a car of only 750cc and created a sensation, amply fulfilling the expectations raised in the Company's new slogan, 'Safety Fast!'.

Kimber quickly seized the opportunity to launch a new model based on EX 120. The C Type was nothing less than a production racing car. For only £345 ($1725) supercharged or £295 ($1475) unblown the less wealthy enthusiast could buy a potential class winner, though after six months these prices rose sharply to £575 ($2875) and £490 ($2450) respectively. Though based on the record breaking engine the C unit was considerably altered in the interests of reliability, dimensions being changed to 57mm × 73mm (746cc). The supercharged car developed a healthy 53bhp at 6500rpm, the unblown version 38bhp at the same revs. Later unblown Cs were given a redesigned cylinder head boosting power to 45bhp. Early cars had pretty boat tail bodies featuring streamlined radiator cowling. Driver and intrepid passenger were protected from the elements by a pair of rather exaggerated humps rising from the firewall.

No less than fourteen MGs had been entered into the 1931 Brooklands Double Twelve, and due to almost superhuman effort on the part of the MG workforce just two months after the C had been no more than an idea in Kimber's mind the fourteen cars were lined up under starter 'Ebby' Ebblewhite's orders.

Results were spectacular. Before the eyes of almost the complete MG workforce the neat little C Type Montlhéry Midgets, to give them their full title, took the first five places, the Earl of March/Chris Staniland car winning outright. The Team Prize obviously went to MG.

During the remainder of that momentous year the string of victories continued. First, second and third and Team Prize were collected in Dublin's Saorstat Cup Race together with a first and third in the Irish Grand Prix. Another first, third and Team Prize were scored in the classic Tourist Trophy in Ulster while in the Brooklands 500 Mile race Eddie Hall almost beat the handicappers, coming home third and winning his class at an average of almost 94mph.

Meanwhile on the production side the ageing M had been lightly revised and a metal paneled version made available at £20 more than the fabric body. Kimber and his associates had also been working on two new models. The D type had an 84-inch version of the C Type chassis (later increased to 86 inches) carrying either a four seat tourer or two door closed coupe body. It was both cramped and underpowered for under the impressively louvered hood rested nothing more exciting than the old M engine, complete with three speed transmission, though this was now operated by remote control.

Of more interest was the 12/70 Magna, first of a breed of small sixes though the familiar dimensions of 57mm × 83mm at once gave the initiated the clue that it was only an M engine with two cylinders added. In fact it was a slightly disguised Wolseley Hornet engine. Retaining the earlier valve timing, 37bhp at 4100rpm was realized. Gear changing was effected by a pleasant four speed remote controlled transmission. Performance was unimpressive.

In many ways it is difficult today to form a fair assessment of the cars of this period. British road test reports of the day were bland in the extreme, and even the most careful reading between the lines seldom gives the clue that the car in question was anything less than perfect, though foreign cars were occasionally the subject of mild criticism. Despite the eulogies heaped on it by *The Autocar*, the Magna wasn't viewed with altogether universal favor. Sneers of the *cognoscenti* that it was undergeared and underpowered with a propensity to mechanical failure were to a certain extent supported by owners' experiences. Early examples suffered some distressing maladies, notably in the transmission and

back axle. Problems in these areas were frequently the result of ill usage during that peculiar form of motor sport, popular in Britain at the time, known affectionately as 'mud plugging'. This involved aiming your car up the steepest, muddiest incline the organizers could find and reaching the top of a laid out course in a shorter time than your competitors. The popularity of this masochistic pastime was why most British sportscars of the period were so pathetically low geared.

Yet the Magna achieved considerable favor, and was bought by a number of celebrities including Prince Ali Khan, Lord Howe, the Earl of March and the famous Siamese racing driver, Prince Birabongse, or Bira. MG were becoming fashionable! Some 250 were sold at prices ranging from £250 ($1250) to £289 ($1445) between late 1931 and late 1932. The F2 was a two seat sports model, while F1 and F3 Magnas carried four-seat bodywork, both open and closed. They became popular with coachbuilders, many small concerns including Jarvis, Abbey, University Motors, (MG's London distributor) Martin Walter, Stiles and Farnham's E D Abbott building on this chassis. Even Windover, one of the great names in English coachbuilding constructed a pair of highly attractive coupes to the design of Lord Portarlington.

In the late summer EX 120 was again taken to Montlhéry where Eyston took the coveted 'Hour' record, covering 101.28 miles in the hour. After achieving this the tiny record breaker burst into flames on its return to the start, literally going out in a blaze of glory. Eyston managed to extricate himself from the tight fitting cockpit to bale out at over 60mph, but miraculously he escaped without serious injury. In December a new streamlined 750cc record breaker, EX 127, nick-named the Magic Midget, made the by now customary winter visit to Montlhéry, where Ernest Eldridge, somewhat unsuitably clad in a lounge suit covered 5 kilometers at 110.28mph, raised on December 22 to 114.47mph by the now recovered Eyston.

Although 1931 had been a sensational year for MG on the racing and record breaking front, sales had been disappointing. The Depression accounted in part for this but it also had to be admitted that production MGs lacked the glamor of their racing brethren. So Kimber set about designing suitable replacements.

In the meantime the C had acquired a new crossflow cylinder head giving an 18% power increase, at the same time losing its radiator cowling and boat tail, which was replaced by a slab fuel tank on which was hung the spare wheel. Teething problems with the new head prevented a repetition of the previous season's victories though Norman Black managed a third place in the Brooklands 500, Hamilton won the 800cc class in the German Grand Prix, and Eddie Hall finished third in the Ulster Tourist Trophy.

In August 1932 Kimber announced the latest Midget, to be known as the J2. The two-seat body with its long louvered hood, humped firewall, cutaway doors and slab tail was directly inspired by the works racing cars. Mounted on what was in effect an F2 Magna chassis it was simple and effective — one of those inspired designs that are right first time. It was to set the trend for generations of MG sportscars

Left: The KN racer and (right and below) the NA variant in racing trim.

in the years to come. The engine also derived from the C. Equipped with twin carburetors and crossflow head, the standard 847cc engine gave 36bhp at 5500rpm and a 70mph plus top speed.

It was an unfortunate mistake on Kimber's part to give *The Autocar* a specially tuned car for their road test. They recorded a top speed of 82mph with equally flattering acceleration. Unsurprisingly MG became inundated with queries from puzzled private owners wondering why their cars were unable to approach these figures. Unfortunately the two bearing crank inherited from the M still figured, this component having a tendency to self destruct at sustained high revs. Nevertheless the J2 was an immediate success, selling at a shade under £200 ($997). The accompanying J1 was the inevitable cramped little four-seat tourer.

During this period Kimber had also been working on a new range designed with Class G (1100cc) racing in mind. These, the Magnettes, were to be produced over the next four years in a bewildering variety of permutations ranging from four-door saloons to out and out racing cars.

First series to be introduced was the K Type, available in two chassis lengths; the K1 with a wheelbase of no less than 108 inches, and the K2, the chassis of which was essentially a widened J2, track in each case being 48 inches. The 1087cc six-cylinder engine was similar to that of the Magna though it followed the practise instituted with the C in having a crossflow cylinder head.

The K1 was offered either as a four-seat tourer or as an attractively styled compact four-door swept tail pillarless saloon with oval lights let into the sun roof, a feature common to most closed bodied MGs since the days of the little M Type Salonette. Elegantly swept fenders of the type destined to become familiar on succeeding generations of Midgets and which now featured throughout the range added a charmingly rakish air. The K1 Magnette could be had with either a four-speed 'crash' transmission and the twin carburetor 41bhp KB engine, or with the Wilson preselector transmission and the triple carburetor KA engine. Owing to the idiosyncracies of the Wilson transmission a milder valve timing was necessary in the interests of even idling, and this was responsible for the inadequate output of only 38bhp. From the middle of 1933 the K1 was much improved by the adoption of the KD engine, a modified 1271cc Magna unit given the crossflow head treatment. The saloon listed at £445 ($2225).

The K2 (short wheelbase) two-seat sports at first utilized

Main picture: The KN/K3 racer and, top right, the K3 with a one-off special body. Top left, the J2 racer, Cecil Kimber's follow-up to the M-type Midget.

the KB engine in conjunction with a four-speed non-synchromesh transmission. A few later examples used the KD engine with a modified pre-selector transmission with an automatic clutch, a refinement also found on KD engined K1s. At £390 ($1950) the K2 was expensive, however, no more than 20 being sold.

Confusingly, at the time the Magnettes were undergoing their Magna engine transplant, the second series Magna, designated the L Type, received in exchange the 41bhp KB unit. The only other major improvement to this range was a much needed increase in braking efficiency, the eight inch drums being enlarged to twelve inch diameter.

An interesting addition to the Magnas was the Continental fixed head coupe, its striking styling showing marked French influence. Similar in conception to the *faux cabriolet* bodies popular on the Continent it also featured the double spear motif that was then the hallmark of that great Parisian master of automotive *haute couture*, Jacques Saoutchik. Unfortunately it was a bit too much for British tastes, and proved a slow seller. To give an idea of the complexity of the MG line up during this period, in September 1933 the buyer had a choice of three similar two-seat sports cars, the J2 Midget, L2 Magna and K2 Magnette, while the

customer seeking four seats was faced with a baffling permutation of bodies, chassis, engines and transmissions. The J2 had an encouraging effect on sales, which had increased by a healthy 75% over the previous year.

Meanwhile the record breaking continued, as Eyston broke the 120mph barrier at Montlhéry in December 1932 with the Magic Midget, a feat followed by the capture of all remaining Class H records in a J3, the blown variant of the J2, driving in this instance being shared by Tommy Wisdom and Bert Denly.

Although it had been announced at the same time as the K1 and K2, back in October 1932, the most famous Magnette of all, the immortal K3, did not in fact exist even as a prototype until January 1933. Two of these were built using blown 1100cc engines in specially made 90 inch chassis upon which were mounted modified C Type bodies. One was entered in the Monte Carlo Rally, making fastest time of the day and breaking the class record in the Mont des Mules hillclimb. The second went with Reg Jackson and a team of drivers to Italy in preparation for an assault on the Mille Miglia, the classic thousand mile race on public roads in which success had for years been almost the sole preserve of the home teams. At the instigation of that great British

The very rare 1934 ND, of which only about 18-20 were made, using an N chassis, K2 Body and NE engine. A mere seven examples survive to the present day.

sportsman, Earl Howe, Kimber decided to field a team of three Magnettes to be driven by Howe and Hamilton, George Eyston and Count 'Johnny' Lurani and ex Bentley Boys Sir Henry Birkin and Bernard Rubin.

As the gruelling race progressed, the chief opposition in the form of the highly potent twin OHC 1100cc Maseratis blew up attempting to equal the cracking pace set by Birkin before his K3 dropped a valve. The two remaining Magnettes proceeded to shatter all existing class records, finishing first and second in their class and collecting the Team Prize. This epic victory in one of the toughest events in the calender was only the prelude to countless other successes at venues throughout the world. In its class the K3 reigned almost supreme for two years, becoming one of the most successful racing cars of all time.

Subsequent K3s differed from the two prototypes in a number of ways. The standard K2 94¼-inch chassis was employed and though early examples retained the slab tank this was later replaced by a graceful streamlined tail-cum-fuel tank. All K3s had the clutchless preselector transmission controlled by a tiny lever in a quadrant mounted in the position normally occupied by an ordinary gear shift. Ultimate speed depended on state of tune and gearing, but was normally in the region of 110 to 125mph. *The Autocar* clocked 104.65mph at an easy 5300rpm in a car with a tight engine running the 4.33 to 1 rear axle ratio. Another idea of the very real performance available from this 1100cc car from the early 1930s can be gauged by the 0-75mph in 14.6 seconds recorded by Sammy Davis for The Autocar in an earlier example. Peak revs were 6500rpm at which speed the early Powerplus supercharged engine developed 124bhp. Later Marshall blown cars reduced this to 114bhp with

enhanced reliability. Priced at only £795 ($3975) the K3 was something of a bargain, some 33 being built including the two prototypes.

Shortly after the Italian victory came further success on the Continent when Ron Horton drove his specially built offset single seat streamlined C Type to a class win at the Avus circuit in Germany. Another class win was scored a month later at Le Mans by another C Type driven by Ford and Baumer. In the meantime the new 750cc racing J4 C Type replacement made an astonishing debut at the Nur-burgring when Hamilton won his class by an incredible 25 minutes! The end of July saw the Maseratis vanquished again when Whitney Straight's K3 won the Coppa Acerbo Junior.

Here it is worth pausing for a moment to reflect on the sobering fact that these highly successful racing cars were powered by engines directly developed from one originally designed to power a 20bhp baby car.

Three weeks later came what is perhaps the marque's most famous victory, when Tazio Nuvolari, the great 'Flying Mantuan', drove a K3 to such tremendous effect in the Ulster Tourist Trophy that having once broken the lap record he then smashed it a further six times, winning by 40 seconds from Hamilton's J4. This was the first time Nuvolari had experienced a preselector transmission. His riding mechanic Alec Hounslow had some interesting moments while trying to explain its finer points as the little Italian maestro hurled the K3 through the opposition; a tricky situation as neither spoke the other's language!

Two weeks later Eddie Hall's K3 won the Brooklands 500, after which the season was wrapped up by the annual Montlhéry record breaking session. The Magic Midget, now

Right: The forerunner of the celebrated T-series MGs, the PA/B models with which the Cream Crackers began their racing team did well in competition – this one is pictured on the banking at Brooklands.

Left and below: The MGPA – small, fast and more than a little bit bumpy.

reclothed in a beautiful new streamlined body took the Class H Hour record at 110.87mph, and covered the Flying Kilometer at 128.63mph. The driving in this instance was entrusted to little Bert Denly, Eyston's mechanic, Eyston himself being too large to fit into the tiny cockpit.

All in all, 1933 had been another spectacular year for MG on the racing front, but as many other sportscar builders have discovered, success on the track is not necessarily reflected by success on the showroom floor. Although the J2 was selling well, Magna figures were unexciting and the K1 was downright unpopular, earning a reputation for being overpriced and underpowered and of questionable reliability. Buyers had little inducement to part with £445 ($2225) for a Magnette saloon when for £140 ($700) less they could buy a Riley Nine Monaco saloon which offered similar performance, more room, significantly more economy

and proven reliability. The Riley also had an impeccable racing pedigree, unlike the legions of small six-cylinder Triumphs and Wolseley Hornets that were all jostling for a place in this corner of the market.

As noted earlier, attempts were made to alleviate the situation by installing, from mid-1933, the improved KD engine, but this made little difference, with only 80 of these sold against 70 of the earlier model. The somewhat cheaper Magna did better, and 1250 of the F Types were sold against less than half that number of the rather nicer L Types. With sales of 2083 J2s, the moral was there for all to see. Kimber must have realized this but was in a difficult position to do much about it. MG had built its reputation on racing and to abandon it would lose the company invaluable prestige and publicity. This only held good, however, while they were winning, and constant development was necessary to remain ahead of the field. Unable to afford purpose-built racing cars, these had to be evolved from existing road cars to become the basis for the next generation of production cars, an automotive merry-go-round on which Kimber was trapped. Though the company's expenditure on racing had been modest, particularly in terms of the results achieved, constant development had left little time to study the needs of the market.

With this in mind the range was considerably pruned and the cars revised. The J2 was replaced by the improved P Type Midget, the 847cc engine now employing a three bearing crank enabling advantage to be taken of its capacity to rev. A top speed of 74mph with lowered windshield was matched by acceleration figures of 0-50mph in 20.7 seconds, 0-60mph taking 32 seconds. Touring fuel consumption was in the region of 32 miles to each Imperial gallon. The price of the Midget had gone up but was still reasonable at £222 ($1110).

The Magnette range was rationalized, the N Type touring cars being available in open two or four-seat versions on a new 96-inch chassis, (NA) the 108-inch wheelbase being restricted to the four door pillarless saloon, now known as the KN. All used a 57bhp 1271cc engine in conjunction with a four speed non synchromesh transmission, the preselector no longer being offered. The two seat NA was similar in appearance to the Midget except for a gracefully swept tail incorporating a semi-recessed spare in place of the smaller car's slab tank. Another identifying feature of the later sports Magnette was the curved swage line sweeping down below the door cutaway. This natural dividing line encouraged some smart two tone color schemes. Though no lightweight at 2070lb the N Type was quick, with a top speed of 80mph and a 0–60mph time of 22.7 seconds. An elegant if claustrophobic Airline fixed head coupe by Allingham could be had on both N and P chassis.

Though improved in some respects the KN saloon was now afflicted with even lower gear ratios than before, top gear being an abysmal 5.78 to 1. A top speed of 75mph was quoted, but it must have been rather strained, even *The Autocar* hinting that it was more comfortable in the forties. With the price reduced to £399 ($1995) the factory managed to sell a creditable 201 before ceasing production in 1935.

Back on the racing front Kimber had been working on a replacement for the 750cc J4. In appearance the new Q Type looked exactly like a slightly scaled down K3, and was constructed from a combination of P and N components. It retained the Magnette's $94\frac{3}{16}$ths-inch wheelbase but used the narrower 45-inch track of the N sportscars. As in the Magnette a preselector transmission with automatic clutch was employed. The engine was a beefed up P Type, using for the first time a Zoller supercharger, which enabled the use of much higher boost pressures than either the Powerplus or Marshall. Whereas the highest boost obtained on previous MGs was the 18 pounds per square inch recorded on the most highly developed J4, the Zoller was eventually to deliver a boost of 39 pounds per square inch to one particular Q engine, at which pressure the tiny 750cc unit recorded and held 146bhp at 7500rpm! Like the other racing cars, the Q went on sale to the public at £550 ($2750).

Above and bottom left: The 1934 MGPA, overhead cam, slow-revving engine which needed to be pushed to give the best from its 8hp engine.

Right: 1935, and the last of the OHC Midgets for nearly 20 years, the PB, a fast and efficient performer.

The brilliant pattern of the previous year was repeated in 1934. In the Isle of Man Mannin Beg race seven out of eight finishers were MGs, the lone Riley coming sixth. A K3 came fourth at Le Mans winning the two-liter class, and Eyston's special single seat K3 EX 135, alias 'The Humbug' won the British Empire Trophy race outright, MG taking the Team Prize. The Coppa Acerbo Junior in August saw the Maseratis trounced again as the Magnettes came in 1-2-3 driven by Hamilton, Cecchini and Seaman. Cecchini won so many Italian events in his K3 that he became Champion of Italy in the 1100cc class. Supercharged entries had been banned in the highly important Ulster Tourist Trophy so a special team of sports racing Magnettes, designated NE Types, was evolved from the sports NA. Tuned to give 75bhp at 6500rpm and fitted with Midget type bodies, one of the six entered won by a narrow margin.

With speeds in the order of 120+ mph now being regularly attained it was becoming evident that the racing engines had far outgrown their chassis, so work was begun on an entirely new frame incorporating the most advanced ideas in chassis design. This was also prompted by the arrival on the racing scene of the new ERAs, highly specialized purpose-built racing cars whose obvious potential posed a powerful threat to MG supremacy. The R Type was unveiled to rapturous acclaim. Here was a genuine scaled down single seat grand prix car featuring all that was desirable in such a machine for only £750 ($3750). The backbone chassis was strikingly advanced. Designed by H N Charles it was of a deep boxed in Y configuration, the modified and strengthened Q Type engine being mounted between the arms of the Y. Suspension was independent all round employing unequal length wishbones and long torsion bars. Transmission was by clutchless Wilson preselector.

Sadly, there was to be little opportunity for the R Type to prove itself. Such an advanced machine obviously required development in order to reach its true potential but this was to be denied the small team of engineers at Abingdon. In the summer of 1935 a bombshell hit them when Lord Nuffield, as William Morris was now, sold the MG Car Company Ltd to Morris Motors Ltd, placing MG under the Managing Directorship of Leonard Lord. Kimber was relegated to Director and General Manager. Lord was a hard bitten ambitious motor industry executive with little interest in the product outside its profitability, and, like Nuffield, he considered racing a waste of time and money.

No clear reason was given for the sudden takeover, but it was partly due to Nuffield's aversion to racing combined with a power struggle being fought out within the upper echelons of Morris management. Just how cold the wind of change was blowing over Abingdon was shown when Len Lord, surveying his new domain entered the hallowed precincts of the racing shop: 'Well, THAT bloody lot can go for a start,' he said.

Main picture: The 1936 MG PB. Away from the racetrack, and without superchargers all it had was a 939cc engine, but it still gave its road-going owners a taste of life at the limit. The inset picture shows the dashboard layout which confronted the drivers of the day – a somewhat Spartan approach to the problem.

Middle aged spread —1935 to 1939

Looking back on MG's achievements over the years 1930–1935 they seem almost incredible. Starting with only the most humble material and with little financial backing other than that provided by private owners they evolved a string of racing models whose consistent success across the world was Britain's bright spot on the international racing scene. At a time when British prestige was at its lowest ebb MG, with help from Riley, kept the flag flying, and their bravely earned victories reflected on the whole British motor industry.

As development engineers Kimber and his team, Cecil Cousins, H N Charles, Reg Jackson and latterly Sidney (Sid) Enever, demonstrated skills of the highest order. The production cars benefitted from lessons learnt on the track. Today 55bhp is a fairly average figure for a 1300cc family car; Magnette saloons could muster this nearly half a century ago. This in part was the problem.

Since the heady days of 1932 MG sales had halved as the market became invaded by a host of small sporting cars. Although of proven sound design the OHC MG engines tended to be temperamental in the hands of the public. They required frequent skilled maintenance if performance and reliability were to be retained, a situation aggravated by many owners' unfamiliarity with the characteristics of small high reving engines. The cars themselves were tricky and tiring to drive in comparison with the more refined offerings from Riley and Triumph. The latter's Southern Cross, Monte Carlo and Gloria range featured a variety of small tourers and saloons aimed directly at MG's clientel. If perhaps they lacked the MG's purist appeal they provided instead the more tangible benefits of softer springing, synchromesh transmissions and hydraulic brakes, all for considerably less money. An interesting refinement initiated by Triumph was the option, from late 1934, of windshield washers on some saloons, a 'first' frequently incorrectly ascribed to Studebaker.

While the company's future was being discussed the opportunity had been taken to improve the P and N Types. The P Type had been facing increasing opposition from Singer's 9 hp 'Le Mans' and in an effort to combat this was given a slight increase in capacity to 930cc, which in conjunction with judicious tuning boosted output to 43.3bhp at 5500rpm. This became the PB, the small-engined car becoming retrospectively the PA. The revised Magnette, known by the factory as the NB differed little from its predecessor except for minor body changes. The hood line was lowered, and following Singer's example the doors now hinged at the front, while the chromed exterior hinges were extended into styling 'flashes'. The price of the Midget remained the same but the Magnette was drastically reduced to £280 ($1400) for the two seat sports, with similar reductions on other versions. Needless to say, the racing cars were withdrawn altogether from the catalogs.

The initial idea behind the Morris takeover was to reorganize MG into a more profitable concern by producing upmarket variations of cars already existing within the group, while dropping the sportscars altogether. Kimber fortunately retained sufficient influence to avert such catastrophe, but cold fact dictated that the accountants had to be appeased and this inevitably meant rationalization. While it was sad to see the passing of the jewel-like little OHC engines, few buyers would mourn the difficult nonsynchro transmission and frequently erratic cable operated brakes. Kimber for some reason shared with Ettore Bugatti a distrust of hydraulic systems. When operating correctly MG cable brakes had been notably effective, but they required constant attention.

If MG's briefly worded announcement that they were quitting racing came as a shock to their followers it was nothing compared with their bewilderment when the first MG designed under the auspices of the new regime was unveiled three months later in October. The SA Two Liter

Top right: The PA in racetrack trim and (all other pictures) restored to absolute concours condition. The ladder chassis construction and wood-framed bodywork makes restoration the sort of task which a dedicated MG lover can handle quite well for himself, although there are a number of professional shops who will do the complicated work with the ash frame.

1936, and the last of the P series Midgets produced was this perfect PB. It's easy to see why these open two-seaters were so popular with the young blades of the period. No RAF carpark of the time was complete without at least one MG.

sports saloon was a completely different breed to previous MGs, though in its aims, if not in spirit, it could be regarded as a belated successor to the Mark II 18/80. It was a large car; by MG standards enormous. Based on the Wolseley Super Six the wheelbase was no less than 123 inches, only three inches less than that of the 3½-liter Bentley, overall length exceeding 16 feet. The pushrod OHV six-cylinder 2062cc Wolseley engine had been mildly breathed upon and equipped with twin SU carburetors to produce 75bhp at 4300rpm. The chassis was of orthodox design with semi ellipticals all round controlled by Luvax hydraulic shock absorbers. A four speed transmission with synchromesh on the two upper ratios drove the 4.45 to 1 rear axle via a cork clutch running in oil.

This chassis was clothed with a handsome low slung four door sports saloon body designed by Kimber, and featured long flowing fully valanced 'trouser creased' fenders and built in trunk.

An original and effective aspect of this design was the way in which the swage line outlining the upper glass area swept down behind the rear side window in a concave curve to meet the upper swage line delineating the waistline, a treatment subsequently used by some of England's great coachbuilders, notably Park Ward. In terms of appearance and the lavishness of its internal appointments it could stand favorable comparison with the best. Performance was adequate rather than sparkling but delivered with a smooth effortlessness quite unfamiliar to owners of earlier MGs. Top speed approached 85mph but the SA was capable of sustaining a 70mph plus cruising speed for miles on end.

At £375 ($1875) it was a formidable contender in the lower end of the sporting luxury car stakes comparing

Derived from the original 18/80 saloons, the 1936 SA had much in common with other products of the car manufacturing plants which economics were gradually bringing together. Eventually they would become BMC and later British Leyland.

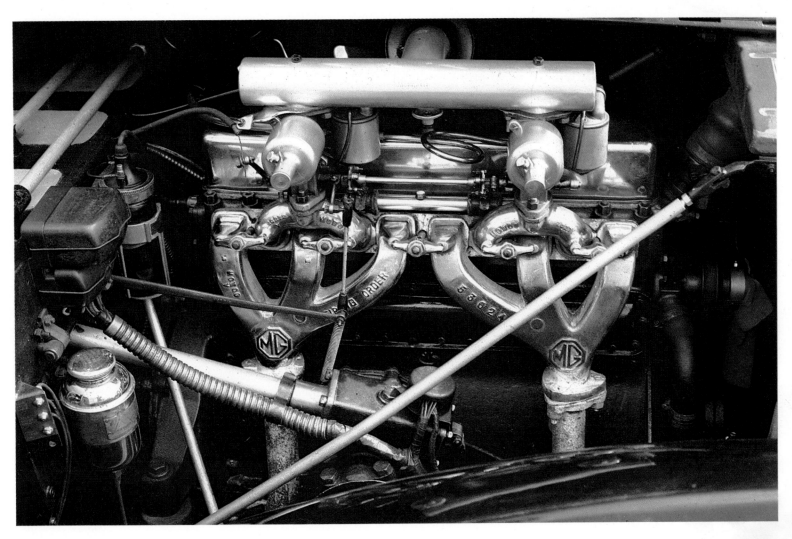

favorably with cars costing twice this figure. Announced just ten days after the sensational unveiling of the 2½-liter SS Jaguar it offered similar performance and better looks for £10 ($50) less and should have given the Coventry product more than a run for its money.

Unfortunately its announcement was marred by a series of blunders on the part of the supposedly efficiency-conscious new management. The design had been rushed through and at the time of its introduction the car wasn't properly sorted out, deliveries being delayed until the Spring of 1936. The five hundred plus customers who had eagerly ordered one were left to wait impatiently for six months or buy a Jaguar instead. Many took this course with the result that in this important sector of the market MG permanently surrendered first place to Jaguar. As an added irony the slogan adopted in 1937 for the Two Liter, 'For Space . . . For Grace . . . For Pace . . .', was, slightly altered, in later years to become indelibly associated with Jaguar.

By the time the first production cars began filtering through they had undergone some changes from the prototype including enlarging of the engine to 2288cc. Throughout the car's production life it was continually revised, the engine receiving a further increase in capacity to 2322cc for 1938. Beside the saloon the SA range also included an elegant two door drophead (convertible) by Tickford and a Charlesworth bodied tourer.

In mid 1936 the overhead cam PB and Magnette were finally pensioned off, and their place was taken by the TA Midget. Though at first subject to a certain amount of scorn from the die-hards, it was far more practical than its immediate ancestors and performed just as well. The Wolseley based four-cylinder 1292cc pushrod OHV unit developed a useful 52bhp at 5000rpm, sufficient to give the

heavier TA a slightly better all round performance than the PB. The chassis was developed from the 94-inch frame of the Q Type with its 45-inch track, thus allowing for a wider cockpit with attendant benefits to comfort. Price remained the same as the PB at £222 ($1110). Further concessions to comfort and ease of control were offered by slightly softer suspension and a part synchro transmission operated via a cork clutch. Brakes were now hydraulic.

The introduction of another touring MG, the 1½-Liter VA, also took place in 1936. Like the SA which it strongly resembled it was available in saloon, Tickford convertible and tourer form. The saloon was particularly neat in appearance and was distinguished from the bigger SA by a fender mounted spare and the absence of any swage lines. The chassis was of similar orthodox design, with power provided by a four-cylinder pushrod OHV 1548cc twin carburetor engine giving 54bhp at 4500rpm. Weight precluded real performance but it was still no sluggard, the saloon and convertible having a top speed in the upper 70s and the tourer recording over 80mph with the windshield down.

Purists have tended to scoff at these bigger MGs but the fact remains that in their day their performance was well up to par in comparison with their rivals. Much has been written about the outstanding performance of the 2½-Liter SS Jaguar, yet the smaller engined SA was only slightly inferior in this respect, a position reversed when examining the respective figures of the VA and the 1½-Liter (actually 1.77 liters) Jaguar, the smaller engined MG being marginally quicker. In the opinion of some the VA was a rather nicer car than the small Jaguar, having a generally 'crisper' feel to it. Like the SA it was capable of sustaining a relatively high cruising speed without undue stress to either car or occupants. They weren't sportscars, but as fast touring cars they

The 1936 SA, as treated by specialist coachbuilders Tickford. This 3-position drophead coupe is one of their most elegant bodies for MG and a lot of their designs influenced later factory styling in the T-series cars.

had a very real charm of their own. Again, prices were highly competitive at £280 ($1400) for the tourer, saloon and convertible costing £325 ($1625). Unfortunately the new management still hadn't sorted themselves out and the VA suffered nearly as much alteration during its three year life span as the SA.

Although the racing shop had been gathering dust and its fraternity scattered throughout the Nuffield group, the spirit of competition still hung in the Abingdon air like a ghost refusing to be exorcised. As racing had been banned, this manifested itself in the form of increased support of 'private' teams competing in the Reliability Trials briefly mentioned in the previous chapter. As these events increased in popularity both the trials themselves and the competing cars became more sophisticated, or at any rate, specialized. Prime requirements were a light two seat body with twin spares to the rear for added weight to hold the back down, a good power to weight ratio, low ratio rear axle and knobbly tires to the driven wheels.

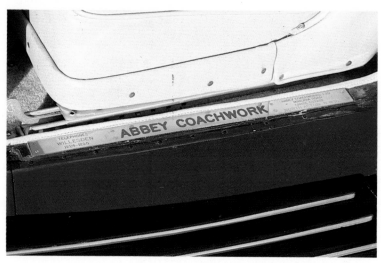

Two teams in particular accounted for many MG victories in this field. The original Cream Crackers team of Maurice Toulmin, J A Bostock and R A Macdermid in their PAs won many awards in 1934 and 1935, sometimes running supercharged. The other team, the Three Musketeers used the NE Magnettes built for the 1934 Tourist Trophy. Driven by Freddie Welch, Sam Nash and Lewis Kindell they collected the team prize in the 1935 Welsh Rally, Sam Nash winning the event outright. For 1936 the factory built three special cars using NE engines enlarged to 1408cc, these being run in both blown and unblown form. They were campaigned with great success by two ex-members of the Cream Crackers team, Bostock and Macdermid and Archie Langley who had forsaken Singers to become a Musketeer. Meanwhile the Cream Crackers continued as a team of blown PB Midgets under the captaincy of Maurice Toulmin. Between them the two teams were virtually invincible.

This was all very well inasmuch as it kept the name MG in the sporting pages of the motoring press but was otherwise of doubtful publicity value. The cars were based on outdated models and further, being highly specialized with

heavy works support caused resentment among private entrants to whom this form of competition otherwise presented a reasonable chance of success.

In 1937 the teams employed almost standards TAs, continuing the previous years' winning pattern. The Cream Crackers won the MMC Team trophy, repeating this the following year with engines bored out to 1½ liters. Similar fortune was enjoyed by the Marshall blown TAs of the Musketeers.

A German, Bobby Kohlrausch, had been one of the foremost MG exponents on the Continent, demolishing opposition in the 750cc class at venues across the European mainland with the Magic Midget, purchased from Eyston in 1934. Before returning to Germany with it he had had MG install a Q Type engine and fit a new streamlined body, and in this form, in May 1935 the little car was taken to Gyor in Hungary where it shattered a number of International Class H records including the Flying Mile at just over 130mph. But more was to come. With further tuning, a special bronze head and Zoller supercharger, power was raised to a staggering 146bhp at 7500rpm, enough to send the tiny car, now wearing its original body, skimming up the Frankfurt autobahn to record a phenomenal 140.6mph, a class record

Left: Although the bulk of the MG output went to the Carbodies' Coventry works, this was still the period when customers could order a body to their own specification as this 1937 saloon bodied by Abbey Coachworks shows.

Right: The successor to the P series MGs was the immortal and much-loved T series. These are probably the most widely known and most affectionately remembered of all the factory's products and – like this TB – many went straight to the racetrack.

that would stand for ten years. This car was later taken over by Mercedes-Benz. Perhaps it's just coincidence that their immediate pre war 1½-liter V8 Grand Prix cars contained certain similarities!

Around this time Major A T 'Goldie' Gardner had bought Ron Horton's very fast offset single seat K3, and impressed with the car's potential had followed Kohlrausch's lead and had it fitted with a similar bronze head; the object being to recapture for Britain the Mile and Kilometer records wrested from Eyston by Maserati, now standing at 138 and 131mph respectively. Following preparation by Reg Jackson and the well known Brooklands tuner R R Jackson it was taken to Frankfurt where the records were comfortably taken at over 142mph. A few months later in October 1937, the Power-plus supercharger replaced by a Zoller, Gardner returned to Frankfurt, raising the records still further, fastest run being the Flying Kilometer at 148.8mph.

An interested spectator of these proceedings was the famous Auto Union designer Professor Eberan von Eberhorst whose streamlined Auto Union record breaker had a few days previously captured records in Class B (5000–8000cc) at speeds up to 257mph. He suggested to the MG team that a more aerodynamically efficient body could result in yet higher speeds. With this in mind Kimber cautiously approached Lord Nuffield for permission to build a special streamliner for Gardner.

Nuffield consented, so the next question that arose was what car to use as a base? Discreet enquiries located Eyston's old offset single seat K3, EX 135, and work proceeded apace. The mechanical side of things were attended to by the two Jacksons and Sid Enever while the body was designed by that talented aerodynamicist Reid Railton. An ultra light frame was fabricated on which the fully enclosed bodyshell was fitted. Railton had recently designed and built the body for John Cobb's Land Speed Record breaker and this was to supply much of the inspiration for the reborn EX 135, now known as the Gardner-MG. Equipped with a Centric blower the journey was made to Germany where the record was increased by almost 40mph to 187.61mph, a feat for which Gardner was awarded the coveted Seagrave Trophy.

On the commercial front sales had grown vigorously since the takeover. Leonard Lord had left after a storming row with Nuffield and Kimber was reinstated as managing director, though he still had to chafe under the tight rein imposed by Oliver Boden, now responsible for MG's affairs. The big saloons and coupes were selling well despite strong competition from Jaguar, Triumph and Riley, and since the demise in 1937 of the Singer Nine Le Mans, the TA had virtual dominance in the small sportscar field. The new four wheeler Morgans from the small factory in Malvern Link offered an unmistakeable challenge to MG supremacy, their Climax engined 1122cc two seater considerably undercutting the MG at only £180 ($900). Though small production took the sting out of the Morgan threat, just to make sure that everyone knew at whose feet they were throwing the gauntlet, the 4/4 was depicted in early advertisements overtaking what was clearly an MG with the slogan 'Safely Past!'

Another big MG, the 2.6-liter WA, was announced in 1938. Apart from a longer hood and wider rear track it was almost indistinguishable from the SA, which remained in production alongside. Using an SA engine bored out to 2.6 liters its 95bhp gave it a top speed approaching 90mph. A dry single plate clutch was employed, the SA and VA also now being so equipped. Available in open form as a Tickford convertible or tourer prices ranged from £442 ($2200) to £468 ($2340) these figures fractionally undercutting Jaguar's 3½-liter range.

New in 1939 was a revised Midget. The TB was outwardly identical to its forbear apart from the 'creased' rear fenders next seen six years later on the TC. The chief difference lay under the hood where a new engine based on that of the Morris 10/4 provided the power. Although of slightly lower capacity at 1250cc this unit was inherently stronger, and as it was to demonstrate, more susceptible to development. Power was up by a modest two bhp, further improvements included installation of the closer ratio'd VA transmission and dry single plate clutch. The TB was also available as a neat Tickford drophead coupe.

In June 1939 as the gathering war clouds darkened

The MG TB was virtually indistinguishable from its predecessor, the TA, without lifting the hood, although purists may be able to look at the slightly shorter scuttle and the positioning of the wheel spokes in order to deduce that this racer is the later TB.

Europe the Gardner-MG was again taken to Germany, this time to the newly opened stretch of autobahn at Dessau. The car ran faultlessly to take various Class F records including the Flying Mile at 203.9mph. The following day, after overnight boring out to 1106cc Gardner captured further records in Class E (1100cc–1500cc) culminating in the Flying Kilometer at 204.2mph. It was then returned to Abingdon for storage. Three months later Britain and Germany were at war.

Kimber's first action upon the declaration of hostilities was to prepare the MG plant for war production. Although the Nuffield group were given important government contracts, for some reason none were passed down from Cowley to Abingdon, a curious state of affairs considering MG's

unique qualifications. This left Kimber to go shopping for contracts, accepting whatever he could get, which must have been particularly galling when no-one knew better than he that they were capable of handling projects of more vital and demanding caliber than the manufacture of light pressings and fuel dipsticks for tanks.

Early in the war he succeeded in securing a particularly challenging aircraft contract requiring just the qualities of technical ingenuity, speed of operation and sheer know-how so ably displayed by the factory in happier days. The men of MG succeeded in this task where others having more apparent qualifications had failed, yet it cost Kimber his job.

Following the sudden death of Oliver Boden in 1940, Miles Thomas (later Lord Thomas of Remenham) had been

placed in charge of the Nuffield group's war effort. Thomas considered Kimber's efforts on behalf of MG to be contrary to his newly laid down policy of centralized control. Kimber was given a terse lecture on the evils of individualism and dismissed from the company he had created. This brutal and foolish action was accepted by Kimber with quiet dignity; the only possible reaction for a man whose talents and imagination had consistently far out-stripped those of his employers.

Since the days of the takeover his hadn't been a particularly happy life. Frustration at being unable to influence company policy had been compounded by problems at home. Following the death, after prolonged illness, of his first wife, he had remarried, this union bringing him renewed happiness and consolation in the difficult days ahead. He must have been bitterly hurt by his treatment from Nuffield, though he never spoke about it, working himself hard in his organizational capacity, first for the ex-coachbuilders, Charlesworth, latterly for Specialloid, the piston manufacturers.

Friends found him pessimistic about the future of the sportscar and the British motor industry; he was tired and looked forward to retirement. Perhaps this was just war weariness, and had he lived to take part in the industry's postwar reconstruction he would have responded with his old vigor. He died on 4 February 1945, aged 56, one of two passengers killed in a rail accident on the outskirts of London.

The first of the postwar Midgets, the MG TC was largely the result of the American influence and was based on the TB. Most changes were under the skin, although the cockpit was now some three inches wider. The inset shows a historical parade, but not in the right order: from left to right TF, TC, PB and TD rear views.

Sportscars for the world

Two views of the MG TC in the setting which most people will remember best and in which it can still frequently be seen at historic sportscar events.

One of the first things to become evident following the ending of hostilities was that life was going to be very different from prewar days. Britain and Europe had been ruined by the war and were faced with a massive reconstruction program extending years into the future. Wartime dreams of an exciting new generation of automobiles to greet the peace were just that; visions, and no more. Faced with the necessity of satisfying the demands of a car hungry public, manufacturers on both sides of the Atlantic retrieved their prewar designs from the attic, dusted them off and sold everything they could make.

So it was with MG. Production of the TC began just five weeks after the war had ended, and by October 1945 some 81 cars had been built. It was little different to its predecessors. The chief alterations were the widening of the cockpit by four inches and the replacement of the sliding trunnions locating the springs by less expensive shackles. Performance was similarly unchanged. Top speed was still in the region of 77mph. 0–60mph took 22.7 seconds and 50mph was reached from standstill in 14.7 seconds. On the face of it the TC was hopelessly outdated in all respects. Its straight line performance was barely out of the family car bracket and its comfort rating zero. Yet it sold. Not merely in Britain where anachronistic discomfort was a way of life, but in large numbers to countries where such a vehicle would normally have been considered wildly unsuitable.

One of its major export markets was the US. It has been said that the TC took the States by storm but with only a little over 2000 TCs reaching its shores this would have been difficult. Its impact, however, was infinitely more far reaching than this modest figure would suggest. Through the TC America discovered the sportscar.

Americans serving in Britain during the war had come across the MG and been captivated by its looks and taut, responsive handling. It presented a challenge, requiring skill to get the best out of it, but once its idiosyncracies had been mastered it was a joy to aim the little car through a series of fast curves, using the stubby gear shift to effect a series of rapid downshifts on the approach, power on and away up through the box, any tendency to over exuberance easily corrected by the quick steering. Light and agile, it was the complete antithesis of the lumbering family Chevy or Ford. Above all, it was fun. When they went back home, many took an MG with them.

As the TC became available in the States it was bought by men like Phil Hill and John Fitch, who used them, like an earlier generation of young Englishmen, as a passport to competition. From one American branch of the MG Car Club was born the Sports Car Club of America.

As the world settled down to normality small groups of enthusiasts everywhere began organizing motor races. These early postwar events were parochial affairs where the

quality of the entries was far exceeded by the enthusiasm of those taking part. For the most part, fields consisted of a mixed bag of elderly sportscars, temperamental prewar racing cars and a sprinkling of ingenious back yard specials. Naturally, MGs figured prominently, notching up an impressive tally of victories.

Although works participation was still forbidden Abingdon was permitted to give limited assistance to a few of the more successful private entrants, and further encouragement was offered by the issuing of tuning manuals advising how to increase the TC's standard 54.4bhp in various stages up to a blown 97.5bhp.

In 1946 Goldie Gardner, now bearing the rank of Lt-Colonel, was back in action with plans to pursue his attempt on the 750cc records set up in 1936 by Bobby Kohlrausch. Before the war Enever had designed a special engine for the job based on the six-cylinder Magnette block with bore and stroke reduced to almost square dimensions of 53mm × 56mm totaling 741cc. Boost was supplied by a Shorrock supercharger. Unhappily, owing to the extraordinarily rigid attitude towards anything remotely connected with racing held by the executive then responsible for MG's affairs Gardner was unable to get any assistance for his project from this direction other than the granting of time off for Jackson and Enever. With its new power unit installed the Gardner-MG was taken, after an abortive trip to Italy, to a stretch of highway at Jabbeke, in Belgium, where Kohl-

rausch's record was exceeded by a clear 18mph to 159.15mph for the Mile and 159.09 for the Kilometer. Experiments made while the car was still at Jabbeke showed that with two cylinders made inoperative the car would be capable of taking Class I (500cc) records. Those in control of MG refused any assistance, so development in this direction was undertaken by Enever and Jackson working during weekends at Gardner's Croydon works. Enever wasn't entirely satisfied with the result but upon its return to Belgium the car managed to beat the existing record by 3mph, raising it to 118.06mph.

By this time MG production was booming as never before. British manufacturers had been exhorted to 'export or die' and MG's export success ensured them continued allocations of steel (supplies of this vital material were controlled by the government and witheld from companies failing to reach export targets).

In 1945 the British people had elected a socialist government and though it could be argued that their handling of the motor industry was no more inept than that of later Conservative administrations the effects of their policies were to be far reaching. Purchase tax was instituted just after the war, initially at $33\frac{1}{3}\%$ of base price, but this was to become subject to alteration. In the late 1940s a double purchase tax of $66\frac{2}{3}\%$ was levied on cars with a base price exceeding £1000. This imposition killed off a number of the smaller specialist firms. For a brief period in the early 1950s this rate was applied across the board to all cars.

Left: The MG TD was greeted with some horror by MG purists when it first made an appearance. Not only did it have bumpers, but the wire wheels were now replaced by pressed steel items.

Below: Count them if you can, spot the different models if you can. Club events of this type are a common feature of weekend race events all over Britain.

The original base price of the TC in 1945 had been £375, increased in 1946 to £412 which purchase tax inflated to £528. This use of the motor industry to control money supply didn't matter so much when the vast majority of its products were being exported but as the neglected home market opened up in the early 1950s it was to make planning almost impossible. Prices could be radically increased by the stroke of a bureaucrat's pen, further control of the market being effected by successive administration's fluctuating restrictions on credit sales. There is no doubt that this constant bureaucratic meddling has been a large factor in the decline of the once great British motor industry.

In 1947 the TC had been joined by the Y Type saloon. This was a late prewar design seen for the first time, the 99-inch chassis employing independent front suspension by coil springs and wishbones, the rear being supported on semi elliptics. A single carburetor TC engine giving 46bhp at 4800rpm gave a 70+mph top speed with comfortable cruising around 65mph. It was an attractive small sports saloon, very much in the late 1930s idiom. Looked at closely, its relationship to the then current Morris Eight could be discerned in the shape of the cabin top, doors and windows, though different fenders, hood and tail lent the car an individuality of its own. The interior was well appointed in traditional style with plenty of polished veneer and leather upholstery. A rather plain, export only tourer, the YT was soon added but never achieved much popularity. It was withdrawn after sales of only 877 against a total of almost 7500 for the Y and later twin carburetor YB saloons. Price of the Y in Britain was £575, hiked by tax to £672.

At the end of 1949, by which time some 10,000 TCs had been sold, the factory announced its replacement by the TD. This used the familiar twin carburetor TC engine in a slightly altered 94-inch version of the Y chassis. The spindley 19-inch center lock wire wheels gave way to the bolt-on variety employed on the saloon. The modern chassis necessitated subtle reshaping of the body. All the traditional ingredients had been retained, including, surprisingly, the forward opening 'suicide doors', but the car now looked heavier, as indeed it was. Straight line performance was little changed, but handling and roadholding were in a different world to the TC.

Despite the inevitable protests of the diehards the TD was a much nicer car to drive fast than its predecessor. Driving a TC near the limit for any length of time was hard work. The twitchy steering could be unpredictable and the rock hard springing transmitted every minor variation in road surface straight to the driver. The TD on the other hand could confidently be driven as fast as road conditions and its limited power would allow. The coil spring independent front suspension gave a firm but comfortable ride while the new rack and pinion steering enabled the driver to place the car at speed with pinpoint accuracy. Added confidence was inspired by the powerful two leading shoe brakes retarding the front wheels.

In 1948 Gardner had taken EX 135 back to Jabbeke for a successful attack on the World Class E (2000cc) record though thanks to the Nuffield Organization's lack of cooperation it achieved this using a four-cylinder twin cam XK 100 Jaguar engine. With a new director, S V Smith in charge of MG's affairs the following year relations between Gardner and MG resumed their old footing, and with factory assistance Gardner set about recapturing the 500cc Class records, now held by the Italian, Taruffi. Having been unhappy with its previous performance Enever redesigned the six-cylinder 750cc (4 piston = 500cc) engine on the reasoning that a poor 750cc six can only make a poor 500cc four, whereas a good 1000cc six should result in a good 500cc three cylinder. Following this interesting principle the bore was increased to original Magnette dimensions of 57mm and the stroke lengthened to 64.5mm, giving a capacity on the three operating cylinders of 493.8cc. A specially made three throw crank operating numbers 4, 5, and 6 pistons was installed, the remainder of this component being no more than a straight shaft extending through the first two main bearings and coupling up the blower drive. This unorthodox approach paid off handsomely, the car carrying various 500cc class records away at speeds up to 154.86mph. One of the three pistons was then removed and the 350cc class records mopped up at speeds up to 121.09mph.

Although this bout of record breaking had been a brilliant demonstration of technical ingenuity its publicity value was somewhat diminished by the fact that not one part of the car owed anything to any current MG, a state of affairs that was to be rectified in the near future.

From May 1949 MG had to share their Abingdon quarters with an old rival. The Riley company had been taken over by Nuffield shortly before the war and it had been decided to transfer production from Coventry to Abingdon. The works was now headed by Riley man Jack Tatlow, but happily, ancient rivalries were forgotten as the two teams settled down cheerfully to work together.

1949 also saw the return of the Le Mans 24 Hour race in which a lightweight bodied TC driven by George ('Phil') Phillips and Curly Dryden remained well placed until disqualified on a technicality in the 19th hour. The following year saw Phillips again at Le Mans, this time with Eric Winterbottom doing the co-driving, where they took the TC to a second place in the 1½-liter class behind a works Jowett Jupiter, an impressive showing which persuaded MG to offer him a special works prepared car for the 1951 race.

Another of the classic events revived in 1950 was the Ulster Tourist Trophy, now transferred to the notoriously difficult Dundrod circuit near Belfast. Here, in vile weather conditions a team of three works supported TDs driven by

Left: The MG TC was phased out in 1949 after more than 10,000 of them had been made.

Below and bottom left: The TD, despite the initial protests which followed its introduction in 1949, soon became the most popular Midget of them all.

Dick Jacobs, George Phillips and Ted Lund took the first three places in their class, winning the Team Prize. The race was won by a young man called Stirling Moss in a Jaguar XK 120. Many successes had been scored on racetracks throughout the World, but these two were to have a particular significance.

By the end of 1950 the company had established itself as the World's leading sportscar manufacturers. The TD was outranking its successful predecessor in the export field and this, coupled with promising developments within the factory all pointed to a rosy future.

Despite booming sales there were two exterior factors in this period which were materially to affect MGs. Before the war they had lost their drawing office facilities when all design work within the Nuffield Organization was centralized at Cowley in the interests of rationalization. Future planning lay in the hands of the accountants, and sportscar enthusiasts didn't figure large within this group. This left Abingdon in a kind of automotive Limbo as a factory building and selling cars but unable to determine their own future.

The second factor was the merger, proposed in 1950 and completed in 1952 between Nuffield and Britain's other automobile giant, Austin, to form the British Motor Corpora-

tion. Since the end of the war Austin had been headed by Billy Morris's ex-hatchet man Leonard Lord and upon the aging Lord Nuffield's virtual retirement in 1952 he took control of the whole vast conglomerate, the third largest producer of motor vehicles in the world after GM and Ford.

It was a loveless union, at best an unsatisfactory marriage of convenience brought about by the lack of male heirs for either Austin or Morris coupled with the natural commercial instincts of big business to eliminate competition by merging with it. In this instance BMC was no more than a holding company, both Nuffield and Austin retaining their separate boards of directors and accounting systems. Efficient control was rendered almost impossible by the distance between the numerous plants and the pursuit of old rivalries within the structure.

So although MG entered the second half of the twentieth century in the enviable position of being the world's leading sportscar constructors in terms of numbers sold, and virtually without competition in a rapidly expanding market, they were at the same time in the ridiculous situation of being unable to take advantage of this in planning their future. There were other sportscars of course, mostly of British manufacture, such as HRG, Morgan, Lea Francis, and in the bigger league, Healey and Jaguar. But with the exception of the latter these were all made in very small numbers and apart from the Morgan, were much more expensive than the MG. Satisfactory sales figures couldn't be expected to last forever with such outdated models as the TD and Y Type, and although they were selling all the cars they could make it was time to look ahead. The car designed for George Phillips to drive in the 1951 Le Mans was to embody a number of pointers to the next generation of MGs as visualized by the Abingdon engineers. Again, as in the past, racing was to be used to improve the breed.

Given the designation EX 172 but more popularly known by its registration number UMG 400, the car was basically a TD with tuned engine and lightened chassis on which was mounted an all enveloping two seat body similar in conception to the 'barchetta' bodies then being fitted to numerous small Italian sports racing cars. This had been evolved by Enever with help from the nearby Armstrong Whitworth aircraft factory's aerodynamicist Mr Beech, who also allowed Enever free use of the company's wind tunnel for testing quarter scale models. The results were gratifying. The aerodynamic lightweight body boosted top speed of the comparatively mildly tuned TD up to almost 120mph, an increase of 35mph over the bluff bodied TD.

Unfortunately Phillips and UMG 400 had little luck in the race, retiring in the early stages with a holed piston caused by a broken valve. Another problem encountered was that owing to the low built body being mounted on a virtually standard TD chassis, the driver was sitting perched on top of the car rather than in it, a situation bringing little benefit to driver or aerodynamics. Much favorable comment was passed on the car's appearance, however, giving Enever every reason to believe that UMB 400 could be a suitable base on which to plan the TD's successor.

In the meantime the TD was improved by the fitting of a stronger clutch and minor engine modifications raising output to 57bhp, thus becoming the TDII. There was also a TD Mark II, sometimes referred to as the TDC, the C denoting Competition. This came with a 9.3:1 compression ratio against the standard car's 7.25:1, larger carburetors and heavy duty suspension. They were considerably quicker than the ordinary product, *Road and Track* giving a 0–60mph time of 16.5 seconds and a standing quarter mile in 20.9 seconds against the TD II's 19.4 and 21.3 seconds respectively. It must have been something to do with the California air because the 0–60mph time recorded for the TDII by the American publication bettered *The Autocar*

Left: The TF, when it finally appeared was possibly the prettiest Midget of them all, even though its lower front and faired-in headlamps represented a considerable break with a tradition which went all the way back to the M-type.

Right: The ZB Magnette. Like its earlier counterpart the ZA (bottom) this elegant saloon car was destroyed in huge quantities by the short-oval stock car racers of the early sixties.

figure by no less than 4½ seconds! The MKII was considerably dearer than the ordinary car, listing in the US in 1952 at $2360 against $2115 for the TDII.

By 1952 British price of the TD had risen from £445 (£569 with tax) to £520 boosted by the then current inflated purchase tax to £825. The Y saloon, now improved by the fitting of the TD gearbox and hypoid back axle to become the YB had increased to £565 (£880 with tax). Handling was likewise improved by the use of stronger shock absorbers and a front anti-roll bar. One of these pleasant sports saloons gained Dick Jacobs first place three years running between 1952 and 1954 in the Silverstone Production Touring Car race.

The Lt-Col. Goldie Gardner/EX 135 partnership was in action again in 1951 and 1952, this time at Utah for the purpose of breaking his own 12-year-old Class F records. Using a blown TD engine he failed to better his earlier performance but managed to capture a number of American National records at speeds up to 189.5mph. Now in his 60s, this was to be the gallant Colonel's swansong. Described as 'a gentleman to the ferrule of his walking stick,' his exploits had enlivened the record breaking world for over twenty years, bringing prestige to both MG and his country.

At this time Enever had been designing a new frame on which to mount a modified edition of the body fitted to the 1951 Le Mans car. Two of these were constructed, one being put aside for future use. They were of a sturdy box section construction in which the side rails bulged out around the cockpit area allowing the occupants to sit within the frame. Following further wind tunnel testing the body was subtly reshaped with raised fender lines and cockpit sides, greatly improving appearance and passenger protection. The original wooden quarter scale wind tunnel model featured side vents just behind the front wheel openings but the finished prototype dispensed with these in favor of two small oval vents on the top deck, one each side of the hood that over the next few years were to become familiar. Christened EX 175 this was the direct ancestor of the MGA. Fully equipped with fenders, top and sidescreens Enever showed it to MG's manager, Jack Tatlow. Tatlow was delighted, and with this encouragement Enever showed it the following day to Sir Leonard Lord in high hopes of being instructed to get it into production. Lord turned it down flat.

For years Austin had wanted to produce a sportscar and at the 1952 London Motor Show Lord had been attracted by the Healey 100 sportscar displayed by Donald Healey. The beautiful Gerry Coker designed body was both modern and eye catching, also the car employed many Austin components including the 2.4-liter OHV Austin A90 engine and transmission, though the weak first gear was blanked off when installed in the Healey. It was just what Lord wanted and he immediately entered into negotiations with Healey for its manufacture under the BMC banner. His reason for rejecting EX 175 was that BMC didn't need two sportscars.

With hopes dashed, MG were left to soldier on as best they could with the ageing TD, though as sales began to flag they

Below and right: The YB saloon was based on Midget components and used a 1250cc engine; it stayed in production between 1947 and 1953 – this is one of the last. And in the same year – 1953 – the TF Midget made its appearance (far right).

were given permission in early 1953 to give it a face lift. EX 175 was reluctantly shelved as the men at MG endeavoured to improve the TD's barn door aerodynamics. The result was seen on the MG stand at the 1953 Motor Show. Many of the TF's present day admirers would be surprised at the derision which greeted it on its announcement. Encouraged by the 1951 Le Mans car MG enthusiasts had been eagerly looking forward to something new and exciting; all they were offered was yesterday's dinner on a slightly different plate. Mechanically the TF was the same as the TDII. Body changes were restricted to sloping the hood and grille and fairing the headlights into slightly more voluminous fenders, the tail also being tidied up. It was still a fun car, but as a real sportscar it wasn't in the running.

Just to ram the point well and truly home their old rival, Triumph, proudly displayed their new entry in the mass market sportscar stakes. The TR2 wasn't as pretty as either the TF or EX 175 but it possessed a chunky air of practical ruggedness that wasn't in the least deceiving. It was tough and it was quick. Powered by a twin carburetor edition of the well known Standard Vanguard engine giving 90bhp at 4800rpm it was streets ahead of the TF in terms of performance, faster by 25mph with acceleration in an altogether superior category. While its handling tended to become a little ragged at the top end, especially on bumpy surfaces, this was compensated by startling fuel economy, average consumption ranging from 28 to 38 miles per Imperial gallon. Emphasizing its potential, the stand was shared with an early pre-production car which with an aero screen and metal tonneau cover and full length undershield had covered the flying mile at almost 125mph at Jabbeke earlier that year. Price of the new Triumph was exactly the same as the TF at £555 plus tax.

The postwar decree of Lord Nuffield was simple – export or die. The TC made its American debut in 1947 and had allowed in many respects for the more refined requirements of Stateside customers. By the early fifties this attitude was even more pronounced as this export model TD, for the US market shows.

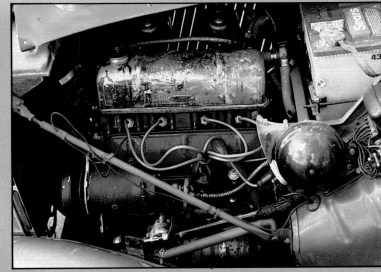

Its effect on the sportscar world was similar to that enjoyed 21 years earlier by the J2 Midget, a comparison that can hardly have brought much consolation to the disappointed MG engineers. The battle on the tracks and in the showrooms was clearly going to be between Triumph and the rather more expensive Austin-Healey, with MG down among the also rans.

The scorn poured on the TF was also aimed at its companion on the stand. This was the new Magnette saloon, successor to the YB. MG fans were horrified at the use of the legendary name Magnette in connection with this Austin engined, Wolseley bodied confection bearing a phoney MG grille. Like other MGs before it, however, the ZA Magnette was to survive the wrath of its critics to become well liked and deservedly popular.

The fullwidth bodywork which it shared with the Wolseley 4/44 had been designed by ex-Jowett man Gerald Palmer now Chief Designer at Nuffield, reputedly following the lines of the Farina bodied Lancia Aurelia, but in fact it

was more similar to that designer's 2500 Alfa Romeo saloon. The engine was derived from the four-cylinder OHV Austin A40 power unit, though as installed in the MG it was enlarged to 1489cc and fitted with twin inclined SU carburetors to produce 60bhp. This, the BMC B series engine, was neither particularly sporting or refined, but included among its virtues surprising potential allied to the stolid reliability of a farm horse.

In its conventional design, adequate performance allied to good handling characteristics and attractively finished interior the ZA was the natural heir to previous generations of MG saloons, sharing with them the ability to cover the ground more rapidly than its performance on paper would suggest. Priced at £645, or £915 with tax, it rapidly secured a firm foothold in the lower end of the middle class market, also achieving a small but enthusiastic following in the US where it sold for $2475.

Early 1954 saw help for MG from an old friend. Following a visit to the US, George Eyston had approached Leonard Lord advising him that unless urgent steps were taken MG were going to lose the valuable US market, and as a first step towards retrieving sales he wanted MG to assist him in further record breaking attempts in Class F (1500cc). As a director of Castrol Eyston possessed considerable influence and was also able to offer financial support to the venture. Lord agreed, so the next step was to find a suitable car.

It was at first decided to use EX 175 with the prototype production body aerodynamically cleaned up by fitting a full width metal tonneau cover surrounding a Perspex blister for the driver's head and filling in the wheel arches, but wind tunnel tests demonstrated that this would be insufficient. It was decided instead to build an entirely new car using the spare experimental frame Enever had had made when planning EX 175 with power provided by an unsupercharged TF engine bored out to 1466cc. A streamlined shell similar to that of EX 135 but retaining hints of EX 175 was fitted and the car given the designation EX 179. In August 1954 it was taken to Utah where Eyston and American sportscar racing driver Ken Miles took a number of long distance records at speeds up to 153.69mph.

This was the turning point in MG's postwar career. Suddenly Abingdon received instructions to proceed as fast as possible in turning EX 175 into a production car. In order to keep interest alive pending announcement of the new model the TF was given an engine enlarged to 1466cc so that it could be more closely identified with the record breaker. A further 6bhp together with improved torque gave a useful gain in performance, top speed now approaching 85mph.

Total TF production between late 1953 and early 1955 was 9600 units, of which 3400 were 1500s, compared with a total of nearly 30,000 TDs. The 1500cc engines were distinguished by the prefix XPEG, the prefix XPAG signifying the 1250cc engine.

Two signs augured well for the future. Towards the end of 1954 full drawing office facilities were installed at Abingdon, and following Jack Tatlow's departure his position as Abingdon's General Manager had been taken by arch MG enthusiast John Thornley, who had been with the company since M Type days. Way back in 1931 he had helped found the MG Car Club and in the early post war years had written what still remains one of the classic books on the marque, 'Maintaining the Breed.'

Above left and above: The TF in 1955. By now its new elegance had been accepted by most people and was no longer thought of as a TD with its face pushed in, as it had once been described.

Right: With the screen folded onto the hood scuttle the TF demonstrates an air of purposeful attack which was not so evident in the earlier, more traditionally elegant models.

Growth industry from A to B

Forced into a rethink by the growing dominance of the Austin-Healeys, which at first were not expected to catch on at all, the MGA replaced the TF in 1955 and eventually brought MG owners back into contact with the twin-cam layout they had begun with. The inset picture is Dick Jacobs' twin-cam MGA racer.

THE FROLESWORTH MOTOR HOUSE WESTWOOD PORTWAY GROUP

THE FROLESWORTH
MOTOR HOUSE

WESTWOOD PORTWAY

50

An indication of the growing importance attached by BMC to competition was the establishing of a fully fledged Competitions Department at Abingdon under Marcus Chambers where in future all BMC works cars would be prepared. One of their first jobs was to prepare three cars for the 1955 Le Mans race.

The announcement of the new MG was planned with a flair that would have done credit to Cecil Kimber himself. The original idea had been to unveil the car in the weeks immediately preceding Le Mans, but hold ups in the supply of bodyshells meant this had to be changed. Instead, the public were given tantalizing descriptions in the world's motoring press of the Le Mans team cars, known generically as EX 182, together with broad hints that something very similar would soon be in the showrooms. At the same time it was made clear that the factory were not looking for spectacular results but would content themselves with a demonstration of high speed reliability, the stated object being to average 80mph over the 24 hours.

Unhappily the race was marred by the worst accident in motor racing history when Pierre Levegh's Mercedes flew into the packed crowd with appalling results. At almost the same moment Dick Jacobs crashed his MG at White House corner, seriously injuring himself. The race continued, to be won by Jaguar after Mercedes withdrew. The remaining two MGs had acquitted themselves well, coming home 5th and 6th in their class at average speeds of 86.17mph and 81.97mph behind the much faster, more sophisticated Porsches and an OSCA. In view of the tragedy clouding the event nobody felt like making any capital out of the results, but the MGs creditable performance could hardly go unnoticed.

Their next outing was to have been the Alpine Rally but this, along with other events, was cancelled in deference to the public's sense of shock over the Le Mans accident. One of the team cars, road equipped in fully rally trim, was tested by Autosport's John Bolster whose glowing report can only have refueled MG enthusiasts' desire to get their hands on one. Bolster ended his report with the prophetic sentence: 'The MG EX 182 is by far the best car that has ever come out of Abingdon. I am sure that as soon as the production version is available the rustle of cheques being signed will be heard throughout the World.'

A team of three were entered for the Ulster Tourist Trophy at Dundrod in September, one having the normal BMC B series pushrod OHV engine as used at Le Mans, the remaining two each being powered by different twin overhead cam experimental engines, one from the Austin drawing office, the other by Morris. These retired, the OHV car repeating the Le Mans performance to come 4th in its class behind the works Porsches. Sadly, this race was also the scene of a horrific multiple accident in which two drivers got burnt to death, another crashing fatally in the later stages. Understandably, perhaps, following on the heels of the Le Mans tragedy, this caused a public outcry against motor racing in which emotion rather got the better of common sense, to the immediate detriment of the sport. Although no MGs had been involved in either of the accidents at Dundrod the factory thought it prudent to withdraw from direct participation in racing.

A sad casualty of this decision was EX 186, an exciting project for a true racing MGA. This comprised a lightened MGA chassis with de Dion rear powered by a prototype twin cam engine. On this was mounted a beautiful lightweight alloy body reminiscent of a scaled down Mercedes-Benz 300SLR. Unhappily, the only prototype was broken up and no photographs remain, the only existing evidence of its ever having been made being a wooden scale model.

In the week following the TT the long awaited production

Above: The guise in which most people saw or owned the MGA, with its 1500cc engine, and in which it became one of the classic sportscars of the fifties.

Left and facing page: the record breaker – EX 181 – in which Stirling Moss took the 1500cc flying mile speed record in 1957, at a speed of 245.6mph – more than four miles a minute. EX 181 is in the BL Heritage Museum at Syon Park.

Right: The road-going MGA stayed in production for nearly ten years after its development from one of the experimental record-breakers, EX 175, and first came with the new B-series engine. The twin-cam engine which had powered the record-breaker EX 181 became available in road cars shortly afterwards. The MGA debut was preceded by a team of three lightweight cars – designated EX 182 – which went to Le Mans in June of 1955. With enclosed coupe bodywork they looked less like the MGA than its successor, the MGB GT. Sadly the twin-cam 1500 cc engine which powered the MGA never made the transition to the MGB.

edition of EX 182 was unveiled to world wide acclaim. It had at last received official designation as the MGA, a logical if not particularly inspired nomenclature, MG having gone through the alphabet, although it was also suggestive of a new beginning after five years in the doldrums. The MGA could truly be said to be race bred in all respects, differing very little from the team cars. The B series engine was detuned from 81bhp to 68bhp and the shapely bodywork made of steel instead of aluminum, although this material was used for doors, hood and trunk lid. A wider ratio transmission was employed with a rear axle ratio of 4.3:1, giving a top speed in the upper nineties. Demonstrating the advantages of efficient streamlining the MGA required 27% less power than the TF in order to maintain 60mph with attendant benefits to fuel consumption, this averaging out at around 27mpg driven hard.

The frame was unchanged, and was the same as that used in the works cars and also the record breaking EX 179. It was both immensely strong and rigid, giving the car handling capabilities far in excess of the potential afforded by its 68bhp. Handling and roadholding were universally

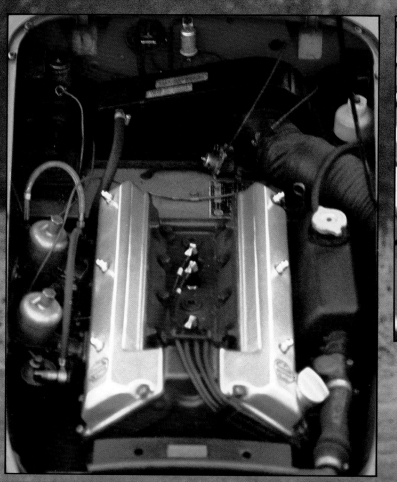

A classic portfolio shot for any MG enthusiast – the MGA shown to its best advantage. Insets show the twin-cam 1500 cc engine and the stylish rear end.

praised. Owners of MGAs never had to concern themselves with the esoteric mysteries of over and understeer; their cars just went where they were pointed. It was the safest car in the world on which to learn the techniques of high speed cornering being predictable, easily controlled and utterly forgiving.

Introduced at £595 (£844 with tax) it was a little cheaper than the rival Triumph, now slightly altered to become the TR3 at a basic price of £625. It was an immediate success, with 13,000 sold in the first year, most of these going to the US where they were offered at $2195 against $2625 for the Triumph. Power was soon increased to 72bhp and at the end of 1956 the MGA roadster was joined by a pretty fixed head coupe which allowed draft free sportscar motoring at the expense of a somewhat noisy interior. Better aerodynamics made a genuine 100mph attainable and the price was £699 plus tax, or $2620 in the States.

A team of three works-prepared MGAs were sponsored by the American MG distributors for the important Sebring Twelve Hour Race where they won the Team Prize, bettering this performance during the following year's event to take first and second in their class, again coming away with the Team Prize. The MGA also scored numerous successes in International rallying including a class one, two, three and Team Prize in the 1955 Scottish Rally, following this with a similar result in the 1956 British RAC Rally, while Nancy Mitchell drove both MGA and Magnette to win the Ladies European Rally Championship that year.

In the meantime the ZA Magnette had achieved an enthusiastic following, selling nearly 13,000 before being lightly revised to become the ZB. This involved raising power to 68bhp and fitting a higher ratio rear axle. The only exterior change was the substituting of the ZA's curved front fender chrome moulding for a straight one. In late 1956 the ZB was further altered by an enlarged rear window and a tasteless duo color scheme in which guise it was lamentably christened the Varitone.

The Magnettes had been proving a force to be reckoned with in both rallying and saloon car racing. In 1955 a team of three showed the way with a class one, two, three in the Silverstone Production Car Race. Following recovery from his Le Mans accident Dick Jacobs ran a successful team of three Magnettes which included among their triumphs coming first in their class in the British Racing and Sports Car Club's Saloon Car Championship in 1958.

In August that year one of the experimental twin cam engines used in the previous year's TT was installed in EX 179 for a fresh bout of record breaking at Utah. It will be

Left: the MGA 1600 cc racer and, right, the road-going version of the same car.

Below: Pinin Farina's prototype for an MG two-seater based on Alec Issigonis' Mini and treated as a possible replacement for the MGA. Fortunately Cooper had already produced plans for a high-performance version of the Mini and this project was stillborn; Abingdon's own (and earlier) ADO 34 eventually became the MGB.

recalled that two different twin cam engines had been used in the ill fated Irish event, one entirely new, the other based on the well tried B series unit, and it was with this that the attempt was to be made. With the compression ratio raised to 9.3:1, running unsupercharged on pump fuel, Ken Miles and Johnny Lockett drove the car to such good effect that they captured no less than sixteen 1500cc class records at speeds up to 170.15mph, including the Twelve Hour record at 141.71mph. With an engine and chassis so closely allied to the production car this was an outstanding performance, though BMC advertising claims that the records were taken by 'a special bodied MGA' were perhaps stretching the truth a fraction!

This was a busy, stimulating period for Abingdon where something approaching the atmosphere of the glorious days of the 1930s was being regenerated. The Competitions Department was a hive of industry as preparation was made for what was to be one of the most consistently successful assaults on the international rally scene by any works team, although it was to be the big Austin-Healeys that were destined to star in this field. Riley production was now being phased out at Abingdon at the last of the 'real' Rileys employing the famous twin high camshaft engine gave way to Cowley built badge engineered Wolseleys, to the infinite

disgust of Riley enthusiasts, their place being taken by Austin-Healey.

In 1957 an important series of record attempts was made at Utah using two cars. EX 179 had been re-engined to take records in the 1000cc class in both blown and unblown forms. These units were tuned editions of BMC's A series four-cylinder pushrod OHV 948cc engine as used in the Morris Minor and Austin A35. Driven by Tommy Wisdom, Phil Hill and David Ash no fewer than nine international and fifty-six American national records were taken at speeds from 118.3 for the twelve hour record using the unsupercharged engine to a flying mile at 143.47mph in blown form. A surprising aspect of the twelve hour high speed marathon was the astonishingly low fuel consumption, this working out at almost fifty miles per gallon!

But this was only the appetizer. Accompanying EX 179 to Utah was a brand new MG record breaker which had been given the designation EX 181. Designed by Syd Enever it was a masterpiece of its kind. The chassis featured a ladder type frame on which was grafted an MGA front suspension, the de Dion rear axle being supported by quarter elliptics and located by radius arms working in parallel with the springs. Braking was effected by a single air cooled rear disk brake, cooling air being ducted onto it from a flap in the body

paneling which opened automatically each time the driver applied the brake. The car was powered by a blown version of the 1500cc twin cam engine used in EX 179 the previous year. Using a Shorrock supercharger giving a boost of 32 pounds per square inch 290bhp was developed at 7300rpm, a spare engine reportedly developing 303bhp, a specific output of 200bhp per liter. All this ingenious machinery was encased within a teardrop shaped shell of almost perfect aerodynamic form standing no more than $38\frac{1}{4}$ inches high with an aerodynamic efficiency calculated as being 30% better than that of EX 179. Unlike previous MG record breakers the driver sat well forward ahead of the engine.

The aim was to raise the existing record already held by MG since 1939 when the 1100cc Magnette engine with which Gardner and EX 135 had taken records up to 203.5mph had overnight been bored out to 1106cc to also capture 1500cc class records at speeds up to 204.2mph. EX 181 had been designed to raise this figure by a substantial margin. Directing the exercise was George Eyston with drivers Phil Hill and Stirling Moss.

Recent heavy rain had flooded the course but as it dried out Hill made a couple of warming up runs on Sunday August 18. He found the car safe and stable and capable of handling higher speeds than the target figure of 250mph, but had a few anxious moments on his last run as petrol fumes flooded the cockpit almost rendering him unconscious. On Tuesday Moss arrived fresh from a victory at Pescara but more rain held off further attempts until the morning of Friday 23 August. Transmission and plug problems attended the first run, and it wasn't until the sun was going down behind the mountains that the car was ready, although by this time it was thought better to leave the attempt until the following day. Moss thought otherwise, and with Eyston's permission climbed into the small metallic green projectile for another run. This time EX 181 ran perfectly, the 18-year-old record being raised by over 40mph to 245.64mph.

Two years later EX 181 returned to Utah with an engine enlarged to 1506cc for attempts on Class E (2000cc) records. Driven by Phil Hill it took records at speeds up to 254.91mph, to become the fastest ever MG.

In the summer of 1958 MG enthusiasts were given the opportunity of driving behind a production version of the record breaking engine with the introduction of the MGA Twin Cam. Engine size had increased from 1489cc (73.025mm × 88.9mm) to 1588cc (75.414mm × 88.9mm) to take advantage of the latest class regulations allowing for engines of up to 1600cc in place of the previous 1500cc limit. It was a beautiful little engine. With an alloy crossflow head and 9.9:1 compression ratio 108bhp was available at 6700rpm against the 72bhp offered by the OHV MGA 1500. The Twin Cam was really fast with a maximum speed of 114mph and 0–60mph time under 10 seconds. The transmission was the same as that used in the 1500 although the extra power tended to expose the awkward spacing between second and third gears. Final drive was also the same at 4.3:1, an alternative lower ratio being available for competition work. In order to cope with this extra performance

Dunlop disk brakes were fitted all round and center lock pierced disk wheels similar to those used on the D Type Jaguar.

For what was essentially a road going competition car the price was reasonable at £843, inflated by purchase tax to £1,266, although this was a little more than was asked for the big Austin-Healey and nearly £200 over the cost of a Triumph TR3. The Twin Cam was in almost every way a delightful car but sadly its potential wasn't to be realized. Like overhead cam MGs of an earlier era it was fine in sympathetic hands but all too often was bought by drivers totally unused to the subtleties of controlling a thoroughbred engine that would race without effort up to 7000rpm and beyond. As a result it acquired an entirely unjustified reputation for being fragile. The high compression ratio made the use of premium fuel necessary, too much throttle on an inferior diet leading to piston failure. Early examples had a dipsomaniac thirst for oil. The example tested by *The Autocar* consuming a gallon in little over 1000 hard driven miles, though this was rectified early in the car's production life by fitting improved piston rings.

The Twin Cam suffered in two respects. Its high state of tune made it unsuitable for the mass sportscar market, while having been designed first and foremost as a fast road car it was uncompetitive in the increasingly specialized field of top class sportscar racing where it was matched against formidable works opposition from Porsche. Nevertheless, Twin Cams acquitted themselves well in many rallies and races, the model's most notable success being in the 1960 Le Mans.

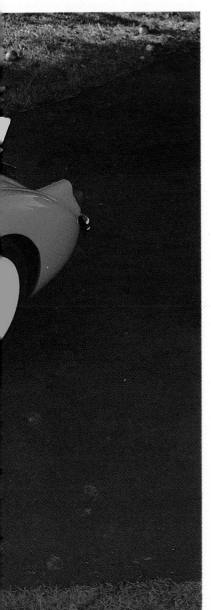

Left: By 1962 the MGA had reached the end of its production life, and the swooping lines of this car and its contemporaries like the Austin-Healeys and the XK Jaguars were fading fast.

Below: Although auto design had progressed well beyond this kind of 'stuck on' rear light by the sixties, the MGB would still incorporate a large percentage of MGA components under the skin.

A privately entered coupe with the engine enlarged to 1762cc won the 2-liter class driven by Ted Lund and Colin Escott, averaging 91.12mph and beating the works Porsches, Triumphs and AC Bristols. After the race Ted Lund drove the car back to his home in the north of England.

Further Twin Cam successes had included a class third in the 1958 Tourist Trophy, now transferred to the British Goodwood circuit, where it was one of the few entries resembling a practical road car. That great exponent of the marque, Dick Jacobs, campaigned a team of two whose 30 places scored in 32 events won them the Autosport Championship in 1959 and 1960, this year also seeing another class third in the TT. Sales remained slow however, and in early 1961 production ceased after only 2,111 had been built.

Early in 1959 the MGA inherited the Twin Cam's block, thus increasing capacity to 1588cc to become the MGA 1600. This raised power output to 80bhp with consequent useful gains in performance. Maximum speed was now just over 100mph and the 0–60mph time was reduced from 15 to 13.3 seconds, in order to cope with which the front wheels were given Lockheed disk brakes. A redesigned top with quarter panes improved visibility and reduced high speed noise level.

At the same time the well loved ZB Magnette was discontinued and a new MG saloon announced, the Magnette Mark III. This time the purists really had something to protest about. The new Magnette was merely an Austin/Morris/Wolseley/Riley clone, all these mid range BMC 1500cc saloons being identical apart from minor differences in trim and state of tune of the B series engine. The cumbersome, befinned Farina styled body made a mockery of the term sports saloon and performance and handling were equally uninspired. It was characterless, something that could never be said of any true MG. The men of Abingdon probably drew comfort from the fact that it was none of their doing, having been inspired and built entirely by Cowley.

Work had been progressing on developing a design by Donald Healey for a small sportscar powered by the BMC A series engine, one of the aims behind the record breaking exploits of EX 179 in 1957 having been to draw attention to this engine's possibilities. The car was introduced in 1958 as the Austin-Healey Sprite, the name recalling a famous Riley sportscar of the mid 1930s. With its cheeky appearance, lively performance and low price the Frog Eye as it inevitably came to be known was an immediate success.

Abingdon had never been so busy, producing a record 41,000 cars in 1958 of which 15,000 were Austin-Healeys. These figures are given perspective when it is realized that the factory still occupied the same floor space as it had way back in the early 1930s when it was turning out around 2,000 cars a year. Mechanization was minimal and each car was road tested before its final inspection. Yet production was to reach even greater heights. During this period Cowley had been developing a revolutionary new baby car designed by Alec Issigonis embodying such advanced ideas as a transverse mounted engine driving the front wheels and rubber suspension. This, of course, was the immortal Mini. MG engineers were fascinated by the prospect of a new Midget incorporating these principles, various experiments being conducted along these lines. An experimental prototype was built and given the designation ADO (Austin Drawing Office) 34. Alec Issigonis disliked it however, and the project was stillborn. Commercially, this was probably the correct decision. The cost of tooling up would have been prohibitive and the car would have met the little Austin-

Healey head on in the showrooms. Further justification for not going ahead with what could have been a promising little sports car was that plans were afoot to market a tuned version of the Mini, which duly appeared in 1961 as the Mini-Cooper.

The sportscar market had in any case been changing over the years as cars generally became faster. In the days when few family saloons had been capable of exceeding 70mph there was some point in bearing the discomforts of high speed open air motoring for the sake of extra performance, but as the speed of ordinary saloons increased the traditional sportscar was becoming something of an anachronism. Sportscar racing had also changed from a sport in which nearly stock cars could compete with some hope of success to a highly specialized business involving technically and aerodynamically highly sophisticated machines which bore little resemblance to anything the enthusiast could buy in the showroom. The sportscar was evolving into the 'personal car' concept as the market expanded to include an older generation of buyers seeking something sporty and distinctive yet unwilling to give up the comfort and convenience of a saloon. Recognizing this, Thornley and Enever devoted a lot of time to more sophisticated development of the MGA, with their plans centered on taking MG further 'up market'. At this time BMC were working on a new series of V configuration engines, comprising a 2-liter V4 and 3-liter V6, and it was thought that these could be used to power the next generation of MGs. In fact they didn't come up to expectation and were dropped, but in the meantime Abingdon had learned a great deal from all this intensive development.

Some idea of the direction in which they had been working was seen in a late 1950s prototype codenamed EX 214. This was a special bodied MGA commissioned by Sir Leonard Lord from the Italian coachbuilder, Frua. Apart from a rather messy front bumper it was attractive enough, looking like a small Maserati, but it was too heavy for an MG.

On the production side the discontinuing of the Twin Cam had seen a few of the all-round disk braked chassis left over. These were given 1600 engines to become the 1600 de Luxe. Late in 1961 all the mid range Farina styled BMC family saloons had engines enlarged to 1622cc, this also being installed in the MGA. Now known as the 1600 MKII performance was only marginally improved but the fitting of a higher (4.1:1) rear axle made for more relaxed high speed cruising. Price in Britain went up to £940 including tax and to $2685 in the US.

Although in some respects showing its age the pushrod OHV MGA was still competitive, the by now traditional Sebring appearance seeing a pair of 1600 de Luxe coupes take first and second in their class in 1961 while the following year two 1600 MKIIs captured second and third class places. One particular 1600 de Luxe coupe achieved notable success in 1962 when the Morley brothers drove it to outright victory in the GT category in the Monte Carlo Rally, while in the Tulip Rally later that year Rauno Aaltonen smashed the Triumph opposition, beating all the new TR4s and winning the 2-liter class.

With the bigger engine and less prominent fins the Magnette MkIII had become the MkIV, but was otherwise unchanged. A lethargic automatic version also became available.

The late summer of 1961 saw the return of the Midget. Although it was only a badge-engineered small Austin-Healey here was a case where for reasons already outlined rationalization made sense. The Sprite had proved success-

ful; the obvious move was to market a de Luxe edition under the MG banner. The Sprite had undergone alteration since its inception in 1958, the frogeye body having been replaced by an Abingdon designed shell of more conventional appearance, featuring the added refinement of an opening trunk lid! The 948cc engine had improvements boosting power from 43bhp to 46bhp at 5500rpm. It was otherwise unchanged, retaining the sturdy box section substructure incorporating coil spring and wishbone front suspension in conjunction with quarter elliptics to the rear.

Introduced as the Austin-Healey Sprite MkII its MG counterpart was unveiled a month later as the MG Midget, becoming the MkI retrospectively. Mechanically the cars were identical, external differences being restricted to giving the Midget a flattened MG grille and full length chrome mouldings along the sides. The Midget also had a slightly more 'de luxe' interior. For this, the buyer paid £472 plus tax, £27 more than the Sprite, while in the US the Midget was listed at $1939. Performance was adequate rather than exciting, a top speed approaching 90mph coming up under favorable circumstances with acceleration in the order of 0–50mph in 14.4 seconds, 0–60mph taking 20.2 seconds, though it tailed off after this, needing almost 33 seconds to reach 70mph and nearly a minute to see 80mph. These figures were often significantly improved by the fitting of one of the various factory approved tuning kits sold by a number of establishments dedicated to making the BMC A series engine deliver more power than its designer had ever dreamed possible.

It wasn't particularly refined, high speed being accompanied by noise from engine and transmission, but it was economical giving around 34mpg driven hard while the more thrifty minded driver found no difficulty obtaining 40 miles for each Imperial gallon. Handling and road-holding were first class though the high geared steering in

Above left: The driver's viewpoint in the LHD export models – a large percentage of MGA production went abroad, mostly to America. The export models featured 'American' details such as white-walled tires (above right).

Right: The OHV 1600cc engine in the MGA. The 1500 twin-cams were faster but much fussier, and gave too many problems to owner-drivers.

conjunction with the tendency to oversteer imparted by the quarter elliptics at the rear made for a certain 'twitchyness' until the driver became used to it, when the Midget could be flung about like a fairground dodgem car.

It was cheap and it was fun but initially lost sales to the Sprite as many buyers objected to spending more money on the same car for the dubious advantage of a little more chromium plate. The initials MG still retained their old magic, however, for this position was soon reversed, the Midget becoming the better seller.

In March 1962 the 100,000th MGA rolled off the line,

production ceasing in June after a little over 1000 more had been built. This was a record in itself, no other sportscar having by then reached these production figures. The MGA had been an excellent example of intensive development over the years. Although maximum speed had only gone up by about 5mph, useable performance had greatly increased, later 1600 models being markedly quicker through the gears and much more comfortable at speed.

The MGA had been a very good car, but a new MG was now ready to take its place. This, the MGB, was announced in October 1962 at the London Motor Show.

MGB-1962 to 1982

Logical development of the MGB led eventually to the V8-engined model, a far happier combination than the MGC had been. The US origins of the big V8 made it a far more sensible export option as well, but eventually Federal safety regulations raised the ride height and gave it wraparound rubber bumpers which would never have this kind of elegance. The model introduced numerous refinements to increase driver comfort, like fabric covered seats (inset).

The MGB was greeted with approval by the world's motoring press and public alike. Although some enthusiasts were disappointed that MG hadn't come up with something as revolutionary as the Mini, few doubted that the B was a much better car than its predecessor. Chief departure from previous MG practice was the monocoque construction, which formed the most suitable basis for mass production in the figures envisaged.

The familiar B series engine nestled under the hood, bored out to 80.26mm × 88.9mm to give a total swept volume of 1798cc, raising output to 95bhp at 5400rpm and maximum torque to 110lbs/ft. at 3000rpm. The engine had been the subject of much detail attention, the bottom end having been strengthened and improved water pump and starter motor fitted. A new clutch transmitted the drive to a higher ratio rear axle (3.91:1) though smaller wheels reduced the effective transmission to almost that of the MGA. Experiments made during the prototype stage had involved the fitting of coil spring and wishbone independent rear suspension, but this had been abandoned on grounds of cost and unnecessary complexity, the production car reverting to long semi elliptics at the rear. Front suspension was a modified version of the MGA's coil springs and wishbone set up.

The new body was not dissimilar to the Frua prototype but had been cleaned up by Farina, losing in the process the prototype's distinctly opulent air to rather resemble Farina's Fiat 1500 cabriolet. It was a handsome machine, offering far more in the way of comfort than the A. Sitting in the wide, roomy cockpit the driver was faced with a well stocked

At home on the racetrack, left the MGB and below right, its small stablemate the Midget – a far cry from the full fendered grace of the thirties and forties. Main picture: the ill-fated MGC lasted a mere two years in production and never fulfilled the intention of replacing the big Healey 3000 which was its design purpose. The ugly hood bulge indicates how carelessly the straight six motor was simply 'shoehorned' into place.

instrument panel and could enjoy for the first time on an open MG the advantages of winding windows. The B was thoroughly up to date without being in the slightest advanced; a natural progression along traditional lines rather than the leap into the future hoped for by many fans.

Performance likewise displayed the same progressive continuity, top speed having gone up to 105mph with commensurately better acceleration. Zero to 50mph took 8.5 seconds, 0–60mph 12.2 seconds, 70mph coming up in 16.5 seconds, with maximum speeds in the gears of 34, 55 and 91mph respectively. Fuel consumption recorded by *Autocar* (the definite article had by this time been dropped) was 21.4mpg but in practice many owners bettered this without hanging about too much.

Roadholding and handling were outstanding. The softer rated suspension caused some roll when cornering fast but ultimate cornering power was considerably better than its predecessor. The rack and pinion steering, controlled through the large, $16\frac{1}{2}$ inch rimmed steering wheel was utterly accurate, enabling the car to be placed with pinpoint precision. Like the MGA, it was vice free and predictable. Priced at £690 plus tax, totalling £950 and $2607 in the US, it was bound to succeed.

The MGB faced much stiffer opposition both at home and abroad than any MG before. Ten years previously sportscars accounted for only a tiny fraction of cars sold, but MG's pioneering efforts had demonstrated to other manufacturers the enormous potential offered by this market.

In Britain MG faced direct competition from Rootes' Sunbeam Alpine at £705 (£825 with tax) and Triumph's TR4 at £750 (£907) each of these also selling in large numbers in the US, particularly the Triumph which was a little dearer than the B at $2840. The Alpine was a rather soggy machine, inferior in most respects to the MG, but the TR4 was a tough, highly successful car with a distinct 'blood and guts' image born from an impressive list of competition successes. The B was more than a match for it when it came to high speed handling, but the Triumph was generally faster all round.

MG's major export market, the US, was also being invaded by the Continentals, Fiat's attractive 1500 and 1600S ($2595) cabriolets paving the way for what was to be the successful 124 Sports, destined to appear in 1966, while in a slightly higher price bracket Americans were discovering the delights of thoroughbred Italian engineering as presented by the beautiful little twin overhead cam Alfa Romeo Guiliettas. From Wolfsburg came the VW Karmann-Ghia, in no sense a sportscar but with a reputation behind it that could seriously affect MG's chances in the personal car market. Far away on the other side of the world the Japanese motorcycle industry was just getting into its stride.

Sharing the MG stand at the same show was a revised Midget, now with disk brakes to the front and engine enlarged to 1098cc, (64.58mm × 83.72mm) power output rising from 46bhp at 5300rpm to 55bhp at 5500rpm. This meant a 90mph maximum with markedly improved acceleration, though a weak bottom end precluded the consistent use of high revs for fear of crankshaft failure. This was rectified in 1964 with the advent of the MkII Midget. Sprite/Midget nomenclature was rather confusing. The original Austin-Healey Sprite had been given a works designation of AN5, succeeding models being known as AN6, AN7 etc. The first Midget had been called GAN 1, the revised car of 1962 becoming GAN 2, though still referred to in company literature as the Mk1. Prices in Britain and the US were £599 and $1939 respectively.

The same show also saw Triumph's rival entry in the small sportscar market displayed for the first time. The Spitfire was of similar engine size to the Midget, being derived from the Triumph Herald. On paper it was more advanced, having a backbone chassis and independent rear suspension by a single transverse leaf spring controlling

Left: the MGC came either as a convertible or could be fitted with any one of a number of hardtop roofs. Of the original handful of lightweight 'Sebring' coupes (the MGC GTS) only a pitifully small number survive.

Below: The smaller Midgets were immediately and immensely successful in 'Modsports' racing, to the point where they became the dominant breed, even being fitted with these unwieldy rear wings.

Left: The MGC GTS Sebring racer in action. Only six were built for this American event, with special lightweight body panels and distended arches to accommodate all that extra rubber. The coupe body was used to replace the lost body stiffness.

Right: The MGB GT II in road-going trim, and, bottom right, John Thornley with his MGB GT and 'that' registration plate.

swing axles. Performance was almost identical to that of the Midget but handling was inferior, the swing axles promoting unpleasant roll oversteer if the car was pressed too hard. The suspension gave an indifferent ride and somehow it lacked the solid feel of the small MG. Despite this, the Spitfire sold in large numbers, becoming much improved over the years. Coming events were casting their shadows, as the Spitfire was the first new car from Standard-Triumph following their takeover by the old-established commercial vehicle manufacturers, Leyland.

Also unveiled along with the B was a new small MG saloon, the MG 1100. In fact this was nothing more than a lightly tuned badge engineered Austin/Morris 1100, the twin carburetor transverse mounted engine developing 55bhp to propel the car up to a little over 85mph. Front wheel drive and Hydrolastic suspension gave the car excellent handling and ride characteristics, which along with an attractively appointed interior in traditional British style made it a popular buy on the home market at £590, (£812 including tax). Unfortunately its chances in the US market were spoilt by troubles arising from faulty detail design and careless assembly in combination with an increasingly inept marketing policy. The MG saloons were of course not built at Abingdon where the standard of assembly was consistently higher than that found in the bigger BMC plants at Cowley and Longbridge. An example of the curious attitude displayed by BMC towards overseas sales was their decision not to sell the overdrive MGB, announced in late 1963, in the US, where it was really needed, because it might interfere with flagging sales of the Austin-Healey. It failed to occur to them that an overdrive B would have more effectively dented sales of the increasingly popular TR4. Eventually the message got through and Americans were also able to enjoy the advantages of effortless high speed cruising at low rpm, 100mph representing only 4480rpm.

On the competition front Marcus Chambers had left Abingdon to organize Rootes competition activities, his place being taken by Stuart Turner. First priority was given to the big Healeys and Mini-Coopers, both of which were carving out formidable reputations in international rallying, the little Mini-Cooper also becoming highly successful in production car racing. Turner's first act, however, was to prepare a team of three special hard top Midgets for the British RAC Rally in 1961. This was the first year in which special stages involving thrashing at high speeds through forestry dirt tracks became an important feature of this event; hardly ideal territory for the low slung Midgets. Nevertheless they managed first and second in their class driven by Derek Astle and Mike Sutcliffe.

The Competitions Department did little with the Midget as official policy was to campaign the model in Austin-Healey Sprite guise, however, three very attractive alloy bodied fast back racing Midgets were constructed in early 1962. These were substantially different from the production cars, having disk brakes, beefed up suspensions and highly tuned engines. The basic A series engines were enlarged, ranging in capacity from 972cc to 1292cc, to the maximum allowed by racing regulations. One was raced by Scottish enthusiast John Milne, the other two, handled by Dick Jacobs, achieving numerous victories in Britain and on the Continent. Their more important triumphs included winning their class in the 1963 Autosport Championship and first and second in class at the 1964 Nurburgring 1000 Kilometers Race. In 1965 the team was returned to Abingdon where they were prepared as works entries, first in the Sebring 12 Hours where one car won its class, then in the Targa Florio where another finished 11th overall with Paddy Hopkirk and Andrew Hedges sharing the driving. The little MG 1100s were also used in competition, Raymond Baxter and Ernie McMillen taking a works-prepared four-door saloon to a creditable fourth in class in the 1963 Monte Carlo Rally.

The first important outing for the MGB was the 1963 Sebring 12 Hours in which two cars had been entered. The result was unfortunate, both retiring with run big ends due to oil surge. This was because of inadequate testing due to an unusually cold British winter when icy conditions rendered high speed trials impossible. Despite works concentration on the Healeys and Mini-Coopers, factory prepared Bs performed well in a number of events. A series of three special works cars were built for the 1963, '64 and '65 Le Mans races. All three were similar, based on the standard steel bodied roadster but fitted with aerodynamic fiberglass fastback hard tops and extended nose sections. Mild tuning and the fitting of a single twin choke Weber carburetor raised output to 130bhp, enough to give them a maximum down the Mulsanne straight of around 140mph on a 3.307:1 rear end. Registered 7 DBL, BMO 541B and DRX 255C respectively each car ran well to finish strongly, best performance being in 1965 when Paddy Hopkirk and Andrew Hedges finished 11th overall at an average of 98.26mph. As a testimonial to their roadability, 7 DBL, piloted by the Morley twins won the GT Category of the 1964 Monte Carlo Rally, a double cause for celebration for BMC as the event had been won outright by Paddy Hopkirk in a Mini-Cooper.

Prior to the 1965 Le Mans two well known Mini drivers, John Rhodes and Warwick Banks had deserted their 'skates' to drive an MGB in the Brands Hatch 1000 Mile Race. This was divided into two heats, the first of which the MG won

outright at 75.33mph, beating in the process a 4.2 Jaguar XKE. Problems caused by an oil leak slowed them down over the next day's 500 mile heat but still they managed to come home fourth, the aggregate results giving them outright victory. The MGB's overall performance in 1965 had enabled it to come third in class behind Porsche and Alfa Romeo in the International GT Constructor's Championship despite having been entered in only two of the qualifying events. The Midget's record was similarly satisfactory, taking second place in its class to Abarth Simca for only four events out of nine qualifying races.

Much improved editions of the 'Spridget', as the Sprite and Midget were collectively known, were introduced early in 1964, the 1098cc having been worked over and given a stronger crankshaft to produce 59bhp. The quarter elliptic rear suspension gave way to semi-elliptics and the sliding

Less than £2000 when it was introduced in 1973, the MGB GT V8 was the logical and ultimate development of the model. There was nothing in the engine bay to show that the car hadn't originally been designed with this powerplant, and the inlet manifolding of the Rover engine was reworked to avoid the ugly hood bulge which had marred the lines of the MGC.

plastic sidescreens were at last replaced by roll up glass windows. This was the Midget MkII (GAN 3) or as an Austin-Healey, the Sprite MkIII. (AN 8) Performance was usefully increased, top speed going up to 92mph while the zero to 60mph time was reduced to 14.5 seconds. Price went up to £611 in Britain and $2055 in the US.

In late 1964 the B was given a five bearing crank engine. In fact there was little wrong with the old three bearing unit, most of the competition cars using it, but high mileage, or thrashed examples tended to develop bottom end rattle when cold, though this symptom disappeared in all but terminal cases as the engine warmed up. The B engine had a well deserved reputation for toughness in both three and five bearing forms, 100,000 miles before major attention was required being not unusual.

In October 1965 MG launched the fixed head coupe MGBGT Two plus Two. The roof and tail section was cleverly contrived from those of the Austin A40 saloon, the angular treatment given to the rear blending in well with the overall design. The 2+2 designation was something of a misnomer and was soon dropped, the rear seats being suitable only for very small children, but extremely useful for baggage. Mechanically the GT was identical to the roadster apart from a stronger Salisbury back axle, the roadster also adopting this component in 1967. The GT was a success from the start offering good looks and performance with a well finished, comfortable interior at a tax inclusive price in Britain of £998 while in the US it came fully equipped at a little over $3000. This was over $500 more than Ford's recent entry into the sporty personal car market in the shape of the Mustang, whose cheapest V8 started at $2480.

Evidently the cars appealed to a different clientel, because in spite of the Mustang's great success MG sales continued to rise in the States. By the end of 1965 BMC were second only to VW in imported car sales in the US, of which MG's record production that year of almost 40,000 constituted a useful percentage. In 1966 only minor changes were made to the MG range, these being concentrated on the Midget which received a Mini-Cooper S based 65bhp 1275cc engine, revised interior and new folding top to become the MkIII (GAN 4). The resulting increase in torque making it more flexible and pleasant to drive. It was soon further improved by raising the axle ratio to 3.9:1 and fitting a stronger crankshaft thus making it a highly tuneable unit capable of producing up to 100bhp without seriously impairing reliability. Many authorities consider this to be the nicest of all the Midgets. Prices went up slightly all round with the exception of the slow selling Magnette saloon which was finally withdrawn in early 1968.

The traditional MG entry in the 1966 Sebring event consisted of two works prepared cars, one running in the GT category, the other, with an engine enlarged to 2004cc delivering 138bhp competing in the Prototype group. The normal-engined car came third in its category to win its class, the prototype retiring early with a broken con-rod. For 1966 the Brands Hatch long distance race was reduced to 500 miles, though torrential rain caused it to be further shortened to six hours running. Under appalling conditions a works prepared MGB driven by Roger Enever and Alec Poole came third behind Bob Bondurant's thunderous 7-liter Shelby Cobra and a Ford GT 40, averaging 73.38mph against the Shelby Cobra's 77.11mph. Another fine per-

formance was put up by Timo Makinen and John Rhodes in the Targa Florio that year when their Stage 6 (106bhp) tune MGB beat many Ferraris, Fords and Porsches to finish 11th overall, winning the 2-liter class and capturing outright victory in the GT Category. The success continued at Spa, where in the 1000 Kilometers Race Andrew Hedges and Julian Vernaeve came first in their class, scoring another outright win in the GT category.

The Marathon de la Route was traditionally one of the toughest rallies in the European calendar, but for 1965 and 1966 was transferred to Germany's Nurburgring where it was run as a high speed long distance endurance event. It

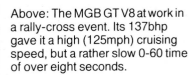

Above: The MGB GT V8 at work in a rally-cross event. Its 137bhp gave it a high (125mph) cruising speed, but a rather slow 0-60 time of over eight seconds.

Left: On the street it was exactly what it was planned to be; a fast, economical and comfortable high-speed touring car which was cheaper than almost all of its major competitors.

wasn't exactly a race, as competitors had to maintain a previously determined average speed on each lap for the 72 hours duration, the emphasis being on reliability, regularity and stamina. Abingdon fielded two entries to be driven by Roger Enever/Alec Poole and Andrew Hedges/Julian Vernaeve. Both cars suffered accidents in the early stages but were repaired, gradually gaining ground as their opponents dropped out or fell behind their schedules until they were running second and third behind the leading Ferrari. In a dramatic ending to the accompaniment of a violent thunderstorm the Ferrari spun off and crashed, leaving the two MGs in first and second place until Poole also had an accident which put him out of the running, outright victory going to Hedges and Vernaeve after completing 5620 miles. Back home in Britain one of the special racing Midget hardtops won John Milne the Scottish National Speed Championship, while in the US another Midget exponent, Carson Baird won the American Class G National Championship.

In terms of success in both competition and sales 1966 had been a good year for MG but it was also a year of changes in company structure that would have lasting effects. Austin man George Harriman replaced Sir Leonard Lord (now Lord Lambury) as company chairman, one of his first acts being to preside over a merger between BMC and Jaguar to form the short lived British Motor Holdings (BMH).

More immediately threatening were the activities of a young American lawyer, Ralph Nader, who was running a vigorous campaign for safer automobiles. Although his attack was aimed chiefly at American manufacturers, particularly GM and their Corvair, the provisions of the resulting Safety Act passed in September 1966 applied to all cars sold in the US except those imported in very small numbers. Another piece of American legislation, the Clean Air Act, laid down a deadline of January 1 1968 for manufacturers to comply with rules relating to exhaust emission. For MG and other exporters to the US this meant giving over a high proportion of their resources to developing means of fulfilling these regulations, a costly and time consuming business that was to reach nightmare proportions as the stipulations became ever more demanding. Delays in delivery of modified components necessary to comply with these Acts caused MG production to drop in 1967 for the first time in five years, though demand remained as high as ever.

Abingdon had been working on developing a bigger, more up market MG ever since the late 1950s. Originally the idea had centered on using narrow angle V4 and V6 engines then under development at Longbridge, but when these were dropped the search began for something suitable. The MGB had originally been intended to employ a V engine, so there was plenty of room beneath the hood for something bigger than the B series unit. Various possibilities were examined, including the Edward Turner designed light alloy Daimler V8s, both in 140bhp 2.5-liter and 220bhp 4.6-liter form. This splendid piece of machinery was capable of propelling the vast, square rigged Daimler Majestic Major at speeds in excess of 120mph; the mind boggles at what it might have achieved in an MG. Rumor has it that at one time there was a prototype running around with a V8 Coventry Climax engine under the hood, but curiously there is no word of any development at that stage involving the Rover/Buick V8. Sadly, none of these exciting prospects materialized, for when it was announced in 1967 the new big MG was powered by an Austin engine. Christened the MGC, it arrived to a mixed reception.

The engine was a redesigned edition of the familiar BMC six-cylinder C series unit last seen in the Austin-Healey 3000, but somehow in the process errors had been allowed to creep in. Bore and stroke remained as before at 83.362mm × 88.9mm to give a total swept volume of 2912cc but the cylinder head had been extensively reworked and a new block and crankcase designed which had seven narrow bearings instead of four broad ones. With twin SUs and a 9:1 compression ratio 145bhp at 5250rpm was realized, with maximum torque of 170foot pounds at 3500rpm. Physically this engine was $1\frac{3}{4}$ inches shorter and 44lbs lighter than the previous one but was still 209lbs heavier than the B engine. Accommodating it under the MGB hood called for extensive alteration to the front end structure. The B's coil spring and wishbone front suspension was replaced by a system employing longitudinal torsion bars extending rearwards to a sturdy central cross member and the transmission tunnel was widened to facilitate installation of the optional automatic transmission. An all synchromesh transmission controlled the drive to a Salisbury rear axle with a very high ratio of 3.31:1 and 15 inch wheels were fitted, those on the B being of 14 inch diameter.

Inspired by the legendary Pinin Farina, there is no doubt that the MGB GT was an outstandingly elegant GT car. Few of its competitors managed to get so much into such a good-looking space, and the five-door saloon has since become a necessity of modern motor production.

The Austin-Healey 3000 had ceased production and viewed as its replacement the MGC came as something of a disappointment, having little of the big Healey's instant blood and guts appeal. Road test reports were generally unflattering and in some cases downright hostile, chief complaints centering around the lack of torque, ill chosen gear ratios and poor handling. The first two criticisms were justified. The engine had the curious and unexpected characteristic of seeming willing to rev smoothly up to 5500rpm and beyond yet the latent power the driver instinctively felt ought to be there never actually manifested itself. This in conjunction with an awkward gap between second and third made overtaking dangerous in certain circumstances, the car lacking power when it was most needed. The handling came in for much adverse comment that it didn't deserve. The C's reputation in some quarters for ferocious understeer was apparently founded during a press preview at Silverstone where, as a result of careless preparation, the cars were handed over to the assembled motoring correspondents with incorrect tire pressures. A lot has been said of its poor weight distribution but in fact it was little more nose heavy than the B, which shared its weight 52.5/47.5 between front and rear wheels compared with the C's 55.7/44.3 distribution. Although not as agile as the B, given the proper tire pressures the C handled well, any tendency to understeer being well within accepted limits.

Performance was similar to the Healey 3000, but

delivered very differently. Top speed was 120mph with a 0 to 60mph time of just 10 seconds, 100mph coming up in a shade below 30 seconds, so it can be seen that the car was no slouch, though at high speeds it was less economical than the Healey. Where the MGC really excelled was as a high speed long distance sporting express. The high back axle ratio allowed an effortless 100mph cruising gait at a mere 3750rpm to be maintained, an aspect of the car's character reinforced by arrowlike straight line stability. Although the flagship of the MG range no attempt was made to dress it up, the only external difference between the B and C being the latter's hood bulges made necessary by the taller engine. The interior remained the same as the B and a heater was still an extra! Available both in roadster and GT form prices in Britain started from a tax inclusive £1,112 for the roadster, listing in the US at $3095 or $3495 as the GT.

In late 1967 the lightly revised MGB MkII was announced with a similar all synchromesh transmission to that fitted to the C, and buyers were given the option of a Borg Warner automatic transmission. There was little demand for this and it was dropped in 1973. Early 1967 had seen the usual excellent performance put up by the American sponsored works team at Sebring, a hardtop MGB with engine enlarged to 1824cc coming third in its class in the GT Category, the same result being achieved by a 2004cc MGB GT running in the Prototype Category. Two exciting racing editions of the C were also built by the works with special lightweight aluminum bodies featuring flared wheel arches mounted on virtually standard C floorpans. The first was constructed early in 1967 before the C was officially announced to compete in Prototype Categories and was powered by a similar 2004cc B engine to that used in the Sebring car though the single twin choke Weber carburetor had been exchanged for a twin SU setup to increase output to 150bhp. Driven by Paddy Hopkirk and Timo Makinen the car performed creditably in the Targa Florio to finish 9th overall and third in its category behind a pair of Porsches. For the 1968 Sebring Race the car was able to run under its true colors with a tuned C engine bored out to 2968cc. Extensive modification to the standard unit included fitting a gas flowed six port aluminum cylinder head fed by triple Webers and installing a balanced and nitrided crankshaft. With a compression ratio of 10.25:1 maximum output was 202bhp at 6000rpm. This proved very fast, finishing 10th overall in the hands of Hopkirk and Hedges. A second car was built and both entered for the 1968 Nurburgring Marathon, now extended to 84 hours duration. The new car retired while the original was awarded 6th place though not running at the finish owing to seized brakes. Unfortunately this was the racing C's last appearance as a works entry, its promising career cut short by upheavals in the organization behind it.

In May 1968 British Motor Holdings merged with the old established commercial vehicle manufacturers, Leyland, to

become the British Leyland Motor Corporation. Leyland had acquired Standard Triumph in 1961 and also controlled Rover and Alvis, so the newly constituted combine encompassed many of the greatest names in the British motor industry. Of the other major British car makers Ford had always been under the control of its American parent, and Vauxhall had been part of GM since 1927, while the mid 1960s saw further American influence in the industry when the ailing Rootes empire succumbed to Chrysler. Thus British Leyland (BL) was not only the biggest indigenous motor manufacturer, it was, with the exception of a few small specialist companies, the only one. It soon became apparent that the merger was more in the nature of a takeover as Leyland and Triumph men took the reins under the overall control of Leyland chief Sir Donald Stokes. These were uneasy days for Abingdon whose staff were acutely aware that they were now under the influence of their great rival, Triumph, their insecurity heightened by the lack of any early indication regarding their future role. When it was announced that the corporation was to be divided into groups MG naturally

assumed that they would be included in the Specialist Car Division comprising Jaguar, Rover and Standard Triumph, but instead they were dealt the insulting blow of being classed in the same category as Austin and Morris.

The little grey men had arrived with a vengeance and seemed hell bent on destroying any signs of individuality. The attitude displayed by these anonymous creatures of an amorphous organization towards MG was perfectly encapsulated in their instructions to the girls handling the Abingdon telephone switchboard. Whereas previously callers to the works had been greeted with a cheerful, 'Hallo, MG Cars', this was changed to the drab sounding 'Leyland Assembly Plant, Abingdon'. The whole atmosphere of Abingdon was becoming poisoned and the spirit that had been built up over nearly half a century was in danger of being destroyed altogether. It took a lot to do this. MG had gone through crises before and survived because it had been run by individualists with a passionate belief in the worth of their endeavors, but at least Kimber and his successors had been able to plead their cause with fellow individualists,

Left: It's almost certain that had the V8 powered versions been available in the USA the production run would have been a great deal longer than it was. The more sophisticated US market needed more than elegance if the B was to compete with the domestic products and the Japanese imports.

Below: The official verdict was that the V8 engine would have needed too much work to bring it up to Federal emission standards, so the badly-needed export models were never built.

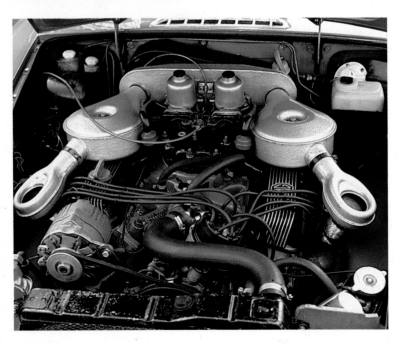

who, even if not of like mind, could partly perceive their point of view and accordingly grant them further rein. It was impossible to come to grips with the soul deadening impersonality of a vast organization in which every eminence was not only grey, but from an enemy camp and quite unconcerned with the fate of MG.

It is of course perfectly true that upper management had a huge amount of work to do in reorganizing an already shaky edifice, and it would be foolish as well as unfair to deny that their job was a difficult one, yet the fact remains that decisions taken at this time, when the future of a great industry lay in their hands, were for the most part irrevocably wrong. Commercial common sense should have dictated that a company having MG's track record would be best left to its own devices; operating on a shoestring budget compared with the resources poured into born failures, MG production had expanded almost continuously and was still unable to keep up with demand. The cars were built by a dedicated team of men too concerned with getting on with the job to bother about striking, and they were profitable.

By far their most important sales arena was the US where their popularity kept increasing in the face of ever more powerful opposition as the world's leading manufacturers fought for a share of this lucrative market. Potent competition was supplied by Fiat who were marking the Midget ($2055), MGB ($2670) and BGT ($3180) with their beautiful little Bertone styled 850 Spyder ($2136), 124 Sport Coupe ($2940) and the elegant Spyder ($3240). Nissan had just arrived with their Datsun Sports 1600 at $2546 and another successful newcomer was Opel's mini Corvette styled GT, sold through Buick dealers at $3348. Triumph sportscar production continued with the much improved Spitfire MkIII, the GT6 MkII, known in the States as the GT6+ and the TR250, shortly to be replaced by the TR6, all of which were selling well in the US at $2295, $2995 and $3275 respectively.

In 1968 the 1100 series was revised and a more powerful 1300cc engine added to the range which embraced both two- and four-door saloons bearing Austin, Morris, Princess and MG badges, the earlier MkI Riley and Wolseley variants being discontinued. The MkIIs had all synchromesh transmissions although buyers retained the option of a slightly lower powered automatic version. With 55bhp available in 1100 form or 70bhp as a 1300 the small MG saloons were lively but all too often spoilt by poor quality control.

In 1969 John Thornley retired and production of the C was halted after only 9000 had been made. Towards the end of a year which had seen production rise to record heights and exports to the US increased by 40% the 500,000th MG (excluding 1100/1300 and Magnette saloons) rolled off the assembly line, though this milestone passed unheralded. At the London Motor Show that year both MGB and Midget were 'Leylandized' by the substitution of uninspired matt black grilles, BL badges on the bumpers and Rostyle wheels, the interiors also being lightly warmed over.

It had been decided at BL that Triumph were to spearhead sportscar sales while MG were to continue building the MGB and the Midget for as long as they remained profitable, after which the marque would probably evolve into a badge engineered Triumph. Commercially this made little sense as not only were MG outselling every other sportscar including Triumph, they still represented the major proportion of BL sales in the US. Also, by the late 1960s development was far advanced on a running prototype which would have provided a highly suitable basis for the next generation of MGs. Conversely, Triumph had nothing ready to replace their

ageing Spitfire, GT6 and TR range and their own prototype, codenamed 'Bullet', was still in the early stages of development and wouldn't see the light of day as a production car until January 1975, when it appeared as the oddly styled TR7.

MG were used to performing near miracles on a limited budget and their prototype, codenamed EX 234, had been designed by Enever with production economy very much in mind. Recognizing that tooling costs for two different models to replace both B and Midget would be prohibitive EX 234 was designed to fulfill both roles. Fitted with the 1798cc B series engine it would be the MGD, becoming the Midget upon installation of the 1275cc A series unit. It was slightly smaller than the B with a wheelbase of 87 inches against the B's 91 inches and featured all round independent suspension based on BMC's Hydrolastic system. Clothed with a beautiful Farina designed Two plus Two open roadster body it had all the hallmarks of success and could have been in the showrooms for the 1970 model year. To MG's intense disappointment EX 234 was shelved on the grounds that it would interfere with other plans and because of the problems associated with making it conform to increasingly severe Federal regulations. But these were excuses rather than reasons as precisely the same arguments could be levelled against development of the Bullet, production costs of which would be incomparably greater than those required to get EX 234 into the showrooms.

An even more exciting concept was the car planned by Enever to become successor to the stillborn EX 234. This was a dramatically styled mid-engined coupe designed to accept either the single overhead camshaft 1750cc four-cylinder Maxi engine or either of the Australian BMC E6 series 2.2 and 2.6-liter six-cylinder engines. MacPherson strut front suspension and a de Dion rear end were features of an advanced specification having all the ingredients of success. The startlingly good looks were from the pen of Harris Mann who was also responsible for the controversial lines of the TR7, before which ill-fated automobile the brilliant ADO 21 had to give way.

In 1970 another nail was driven into the Abingdon coffin with the closing of the Competitions Department. The next year Sidney Enever followed John Thornley into retirement and his place was taken by Roy Brocklehurst. There was little change at the MG stand at the London Motor Show though models destined for the US suffered a small power loss as a result of the emission control laws. In Britain prices began to rise as inflation took hold. Though nine and ten years old respectively production of both B and Midget reached a record level, and it wasn't until 1974 that they were to undergo anything more radical than fiddling minor alterations.

For a long time it had been an obvious move to drop the Buick inspired Rover 3.5-liter aluminum engine into the MGB, though when this interesting cocktail was first introduced for sale to the public it was by a garage owning engineer called Ken Costello, who offered the package as the Costello-MG V8 at £1000 more than the then current price of the B. This induced BL to allow MG to produce their own version which was duly announced in August 1973. The MGB V8 differed from the Costello car in having the uprated

The last in line for a proud heritage which stretched right back to 1929. By this time however (79/80), the MG Midget had been merged with the baby Austin-Healey Sprite and bore no sign of its proud parentage in appearance. Yet indeed it lived up exactly to the original specifications for the M-type Midget.

MGC transmission and rear axle though for political reasons it was given the low compression (8.5:1) Range-Rover engine giving 137bhp instead of the more powerful unit used in the big Rover saloons. Nevertheless, the car was fast, much quicker than the MGC to the extent that the C's claims of 145bhp become questionable. Road tests recorded a top speed of 124mph with acceleration verging on supercar standards. Thirty mph was reached in only 2.8 seconds compared with the C's 4 seconds, 60mph came up in 8.6 seconds, the magic 100mph taking 25.3 seconds. Unlike the C the V8 was remarkably economical for its size and performance, *Autocar* recording an overall consumption of 23.4mpg against 17.5 for the C. The Rover unit was lighter and more compact than the C's lengthy six enabling the MGB V8 to retain the four cylinder car's coil spring and wishbone suspension, so handling remained unimpaired, if slightly old fashioned. The V8 was a fine car and competitively priced in Britain at £2294 inclusive of tax. It was only available in hardtop GT form. Americans had to forego the pleasure of owning the fastest ever touring MG supposedly because the US importers were concerned that it would damage sales of Jaguar's XJ6 and the slow moving Triumph Stag. Given the enthusiastic backing and marketing it deserved it should have been a success but its chances were spoiled by interdepartmental squabbling and it was withdrawn in 1976 after only 2591 had been built. As one observer of the ramshackle empire remarked at the time: 'They're getting so confused at BL that they're actually stabbing one another in the front.'

In 1974 both Midget and MGB received their last major facelift though in neither case could it be said they had been improved. Hideous black molded plastic snouts and massive '5mph'bumpers dictated by the latest American regulations ruined their appearance while handling was adversely affected by raising the suspension an inch and an inch and a half respectively. Mechanically the B remained virtually unchanged apart from American editions which had engines so stifled in complying with emission control laws that power was no longer quoted, though educated guesses place it at around the same level as the MGA 1500.

The Midget, although still designated the MkIII underwent major surgery as the A series 1275cc Cooper based engine was replaced by a 1493cc Triumph unit coupled to a 1.3-liter Morris Marina all synchromesh transmission. Power was up to 65bhp at 5500rpm with considerably improved torque, raising the top speed to a little over 100mph with acceleration in the order of zero to 60mph in 12.3 seconds, but as on the B, the increase in ride height and weight had a detrimental effect on handling. Although the bigger engine made for more comfortable high speed cruising, the Midget had lost its crispness. Straight line stability of both MGs was still excellent, but excessive roll could be induced under rapid cornering, an unfortunate by-product of regulations formulated to promote safety. In their efforts to safeguard car occupants from the result of accident, the safety legislators consistently overlooked the importance of primary safety; the avoidance of accidents through better roadholding, steering and brakes.

By the end of 1974 British Leyland were in such desperate financial trouble that only government intervention could save them. An initial injection of £50 million (over $100 million) was soon followed by full nationalization as the scale of their problem became apparent. The reasons underlying the collapse of Britain's major car maker are complex, their roots going back many years, and involving political, economic and social factors. The ground was laid in the early

1950s when complacent management gave little thought to the future as profits rolled in from car-starved home and tariff protected Commonwealth markets. Their products were dull, unimaginative and generally unsuited to conditions abroad, while insufficient money was invested in new plant and machinery. As Continental manufacturers such as Renault, Fiat, Peugeot, Borgward and especially Volkswagen entered the arena with new models designed for world markets, British cars became ever less competitive and moreover began to attract an unenviable reputation for poor quality and inadequate servicing and spares facilities.

The problems were compounded as large sections of the industry merged to snowball into the vast conglomerate that became British Leyland. By the 1970s there were no fewer than 55 major BL manufacturing plants scattered throughout the Midlands of which 29 were involved in car production and were, for the most part, old and hopelessly inefficient. A confused product range contained too many overlapping models competing against each other, some of which were outdated before they left the drawing board and others, technically more advanced, still only suitable for the British market. A demoralized workforce vented its ill feeling through incessant strikes and wage demands rendered necessary by growing inflation.

The cumulative effects of this downward spiral were further aggravated by the need to comply with the constantly proliferating and ever more fussy US regulations which in 1977 were to be matched by a different set of rules governing the sales of cars in Europe, the European Type Approval Laws. The modern automobile designer could no longer work within the traditional parameters of his craft. Instead it was becoming a matter of feeding vast quantities of often conflicting regulation requirements into a computer and seeing how closely the result could be made to resemble an automobile.

By this time MGs were so outdated that the average family saloon could run rings round them. An entirely new generation of sportscars had taken over, leaving these relics of an earlier age in a quiet backwater of the marketplace where they nevertheless continued to sell well to traditionalists and to those individuals to whom the initials MG still had a ring of magic. Like BMC's ageless Morris Minor, the MGB seemed a candidate for immortality. Throughout 1976 and 1977 B and Midget underwent a series of minor changes in specification including a new dashboard common to both models and the raising of the Midget's rear axle ratio from 3.91:1 to 3.72:1. Inflation was making nonsense of British prices, that of the B for example having been constantly revised upwards from £1,450 in 1973 to £6252 for the last few examples sold in 1981. In 1977 a limited edition 'Anniversary' MGBGT was offered, distinguished from the regular car by a duotone green and gold paint finish, but was otherwise unremarkable. This year also saw the Midget withdrawn from the US, production ceasing altogether in 1979. The B remained available to US buyers until 1980, listing at $7950 against $8795 asked for Fiat's almost equally venerable 2000 Spyder.

Yet despite the continuing healthy demand for MGs, particularly from the States, Abingdon's future was becoming increasingly insecure as the parent organization's convulsions began to take on the aspect of death throes. In 1975 leading BL men Lord Stokes and John Barber were removed from their positions and Alex Park given the thankless task of reorganization. Conditions rendered his job impossible and in 1977 he in turn was replaced by Michael Edwardes, who demanded, and was given, a free hand and full govern-

From the BL Heritage museum at Syon Park, this is the last exhibit to have come from the MG works until the name was revived as a piece of badge engineering for Metro and Maestro. EOL 733V was the last MG to roll off the line when it finally closed down in 1980.

ment backing to revitalize the ailing giant. His survival plan depended on reducing the size of the corporation, ruthless cutting out of all deadwood and complete modernization. As it became evident that Abingdon was to fall before the ax in the cause of greater efficiency (shades of the past!) a number of rescue bids were attempted including talk of a possible takeover by Aston Martin, but sadly, there was to be no reprieve. The small sportscar factory which had seen so much automobile history made over the past 50 years was sold in 1981, while the last cars to be constructed within its walls lingered on in the price lists and a few showrooms until the summer of the following year. Sportscar enthusiasts were stunned as realization dawned that this was truly the end of the line, that there would be no more MGs.

How could ceasing production of the world's most consistently successful sportscar be reconciled with the interests even of big business? One senior BL executive was quoted as saying that the company lost £800 (over $1600) on every MGB sold in the latter parts of its existence, but this is difficult to believe. The cost of meeting ever more demanding regulation requirements was, and is, enormous, but these expenses would have been to a considerable extent shared among other models, and tooling costs for the MGB must have been recovered years ago. Well over half a million MGB's had

been built by the time the last one drove out of the factory gates in October 1980, surely sufficient evidence to sustain the belief that a large profitable market awaited a suitable successor?

In 1982 the name returned, though now the octagon only graces an up-market Austin Metro. The transverse mounted engine is an updated version of the trusty, though ancient BMC A series 1275cc unit used in the Midget between 1966 and 1974, tuned to produce 72bhp in place of the regular Metro's 60bhp. Brief experience shows it to be a pleasant small sporty saloon in the modern idiom with a useful performance comfortably delivered. Claimed top speed is a little over 100mph with zero to 60mph taking 10.9 seconds, making it considerably quicker than the MGB. At almost £4800 the MG Metro faces healthy opposition but greatly improved finish and build quality compared with earlier BL offerings should enable it to compete on level terms in its market sector.

The small factory in Abingdon is still there, but the empty halls that until recently rang to the bustle of industry and the throaty rasping of sportscar exhausts now echo only the creaking and banging of doors swinging in the wind. It is a memory haunted place, but the spirit which created it has gone, and we are all the poorer for its going.

Appendix

1923–1924   11.9hp 'Rawarth'
4 cylinder 69.5 × 102mm 1548cc
3 forward speeds
Wheelbase: 102in
Max speed: approx 60mph
Number made: 6 (sporting two seat body)

1924–1926   14/28 Super sports (Bullnose)
4 cylinder 75 × 102mm 1802cc
3 forward speeds
Wheelbase: 102in (short), 108in (long)
Max speed: approx 60mph
Number made: approx 400 (open and closed, two and four seats)

1926–1929   14/28 'flatnose' and 14/40 Mk IV
4 cylinder 75 × 102mm 1802cc
BHP: approx 35 at 4000rpm
3 forward speeds
Wheelbase: 106½in
Max speed: 60+mph
Number made: approx 900 (open and closed, two and four seats)

1928–1931   18/80 Six Mk I
1929–1933   Mk II
6 cylinder 69 × 110mm 2468cc
BHP: approx 60 at 3200rpm
3 forward speeds (Mk I)
4 forward speeds (Mk II)
Wheelbase: 114in
Max speed: 75–80mph depending on coachwork
Number made: Mk I 500, Mk II 236 (open and closed two and four seats

1930   18/100 Six Mk III (Tigresse) Competition
6 cylinder 69 × 110mm 2468cc
BHP: 90 approx depending on state of tune
4 forward speeds
Wheelbase: 114in
Max speed: approx 90mph
Number made: 5 (lightweight four seat tourer)

1928–1932   M Type Midget
4 cylinder 57 × 83mm 847cc
BHP: 20 at 4000rpm, later 27 at 4500rpm
3 forward speeds
Max speed: 60+mph
Number made: 3235 (two seat sports and 2/4 seat 'Salonette')

1931–1932   C Type Midget Competition
4 cylinder 57 × 73mm 746cc
BHP: 38 (early unsupercharged); 44 (late unsupercharged); 53+ (supercharged)
4 forward speeds
Wheelbase: 81in
Max speed: up to 100mpg depending on state of tune
Number made: 44 (two seat sports/racing body)

1931–1932   D Type Midget
4 cylinder 57 × 83mm 847cc
BHP: 27 at 4500rpm
3 forward speeds
Wheelbase: 84in
Max speed: 60mph
Number made: 250 (four seat open and closed)

1931–1932   F Type Magna
6 cylinder 57 × 83mm 1271cc
BHP: 37 at 4500rpm
4 forward speeds
Wheelbase: 94in
Max speed: 70mph
Number made: 1250 (F1 and F3 open and closed four seats; F2 two seat sports)

1932–1934   J1 and J2 Midgets
4 cylinder 57 × 83mm 847cc
BHP: 36 at 5500rpm
4 forward speeds
Wheelbase: 86in
Max speed: 70+mph
Number made: 380 (J1 open four seat tourer); 2082 (J2 open two seat sports)

1932–1933   J3 and J4 Midgets Competition
4 cylinder 57 × 73mm 746cc (supercharged)
BHP: up to 74 depending on state of tune
4 forward speeds
Wheelbase: 86in
Max speed: up to 100+mph depending on state of tune
Number made: 22 (J3), 9 (J4)

1933–1934   K Type Magnette (KA and KB engines)
6 cylinder 57 × 71mm 1087cc
BHP: KA 39 at 5500rpm, KB 41 at 5500rpm
4 forward speeds (KA preselector, KB 'Crash')
Wheelbase: K1 (four seat) 108in, K2 (two seat) 94¼in
Max speed: up to 75mph
Number made: 71 (K1) (wide variety of open and closed bodywork, 15 (K2) (sports to seat)

1933–1934   K Type Magnette (KD engine)
6 cylinder 57 × 83mm 1271cc
BHP: 48.5 at 5500rpm or 55 at 5500rpm according to valve timing

4 forward speeds (preslector)
Wheelbase: K1 (4 seat) 108in, K2 (2 seat) 94¼in
Max speed: up to 80mph depending on body
Number made: 81 (K1) (wide variety of open and closed bodywork), 15 (K2) (two seat sports)

1932–1934   K3 Magnette Competition
6 cylinder 57 × 71mm 1087cc supercharged
BHP: up to 124 according to state of tune
4 forward speeds (preslector)
Wheelbase: 94¼in
Max speed: up to 120mph depending on state of tune (standard body)
Number made: 33 (including prototypes and EX 135)

1933–1934   L Type Magna
6 cylinder 57 × 71mm 1087cc
BHP: 41 at 5500rpm
4 forward speeds
Wheelbase: 94   in
Max speed: up to 75mph
Acceleration: 0–50mph = 18 seconds, 0–60mph = 24.4 seconds (L2)
Number made: 486 (L1 four seat), 90 (L2 two-seat)

1934–1936   Types PA and PB Midgets
PA 4-cylinder 57 × 83mm 847cc, PB 60 × 83mm 939cc
BHP: PA 35 at 5600rpm, PB 43 at 5500rpm
Wheelbase: 86½in
Max speed: PA 70+mph, PB up to 75mph
Acceleration: PA 0–50mph = 20.8 seconds, 0–60mph = 32.2 seconds; PB 0–50mph = 16.5 seconds, 0–60mph = 27.4 seconds
Number made: 1973 (PA), 526 (PB, including 27 converted PAs)

1934–1936   NA Magnette (including NB and ND)
6 cylinder 57 × 83mm 1271cc
BHP: 57 at 5700rpm
4 forward speeds
Wheelbase: 96in
Max speed: up to 80mph depending on body
Acceleration: 0–50mph = 16.4 seconds, 0–60mph = 22.8 seconds (these figures for two seat sports)
Number made: 738 (two and four seat, open and closed)

1934   NE Magnette Competition
6 cylinder 57 G83mm 1271cc
BHP: 74 at 6500rpm
4 forward speeds
Wheelbase: 96in
Max speed: up to 100mph
Number made: 7

1934–1935   KN Magnette
6 cylinder 57 × 83mm 1271cc
BHP: 57 at 5700rpm
4 forward speeds
Wheelbase: 96in
Max speed: 75mph
Acceleration: 0–50mph = 18.4 seconds, 0–60mph = 28.6 seconds
Number made: 201 (saloon only)

1934   Q Type Midget Competition
4 cylinder 57 × 73mm 746cc supercharged
BHP: 113 at 7200rpm
4 forward speeds (preselector)
Wheelbase: 94¼in
Max speed: dependant on state of tune and gearing
Number made: 8

1934   Q Type Midget Competition
4 cylinder 57 × 73mm 746cc
BHP: 113 at 7200rpm
4 forward speeds (preselector)
Wheelbase: 94¼in
Max speed: dependant on state of tune and gearing
Number made: 8

1935   R Type Midget Competition
4 cylinder 57 × 73mm 746cc
BHP: 113 at 7200rpm
4 forward speeds (preslector)
Wheelbase: 90½in
Max speed: dependant on state of tune and gearing
Number made: 10

1935–1939   SA 2-liter
6 cylinder 69 G102mm 2288cc later 69.5 × 102mm 2322cc
BHP: 75 at 4300rpm
4 forward speeds
Wheelbase: 123in
Max speed: 80+mph
Acceleration: 0–60mph = 22.5 seconds
Number made: 2738 (saloons, convertibles and tourers

1937–1939   VA 1½-liter
4 cylinder 69.5 × 102mm 1548cc
BHP: 54 at 4500rpm
4 forward speeds
Wheelbase: 108in
Max speed: up to 80mph
Acceleration: 0–50mph = 15.8 seconds, 0–60mph = 22.8 seconds
Number made: 2407 (saloons, convertibles and tourers

1938–1939   WA 2.6-liter
6 cylinder 73 × 102mm 2561cc
BHP: 95 at 4400rpm
4 forward speeds
Wheelbase: 123in
Max speed: 85+mph
Acceleration: N/A
Number made: 369

1936–1939   TA Type Midget
4 cylinder 63.5 × 102mm 1292cc
BHP: 52 at 5000rpm
4 forward speeds
Wheelbase: 94in
Max speed: 78mph
Acceleration: 0–50mph = 15.4
seconds, 0–60mph = 23.1 seconds
Number made: 3003

1939   TB Type Midget
4 cylinder 66.5 = 90mm 1250cc
BHP: 54 at 5200rpm
4 forward speeds
Wheelbase: 94in
Max speed: performance figures N/A
(approximately as for TC below)
Number made: 379

1945–1949   TC Type Midget
4 cylinder 66.5 × 90mm 1250cc
BHP: 54 at 5200rpm
4 forward speeds
Wheelbase: 94in
Max speed: 77mph
Acceleration: 0–50mph = 14.7
seconds, 0–60mph = 22.7 seconds
Number made: 10,000

1947–1953   Y Type 1¼-liter
4 cylinder 66.5 × 90mm 1250cc
BHP: YA & YB 46 at 4800rpm,
TY 54 at 5200rpm
4 forward speeds
Wheelbase: 99in
Max speed: 70mph
Acceleration: 0–50mph = 16.9
seconds, 0–60mph = 28.2 seconds
Number made: 6158 (YA saloon),
1301 (YB saloon), 877 (YT tourer)

1949–1953   TD Type Midget
4 cylinder 66.5 × 90mm 1250cc
BHP: 54 at 5200rpm, TDII 57 at
5500rpm
4 forward speeds
Wheelbase: 94in
Max speed: 75 + mph
Acceleration: 0–50mph = 15.3
seconds, 0–60mph = 23.5 seconds
Number made: 29,664

**1953–1955   TF Midget 1250 and
1500**
4 cylinder 66.5 × 90mm 1250cc,
later 72 × 90mm 1466cc
BHP: 57 at 5500 (1250), 63 at 5000
(1500)
4 forward speeds
Wheelbase: 94in
Max speed: 1250 80mph, 1500
85mph
Acceleration: 1250 0–50mph = 13
seconds, 0–60mph = 18.9 seconds;
1500 0–50mph = 11 seconds,
0–60mph = 16.3 seconds
Number made: 6200 (1250), 3400
(1500)

**1953–1958   ZA and ZB Magnette
Saloons**
4 cylinders 73.025 × 88.9mm 1489cc
BHP: ZA 60 at 4600rpm, ZB 68 at
5250rpm
4 forward speeds
Wheelbase: 102in
Max speed: ZA 80mph, ZB 87mph
Acceleration: ZA 0–50mph = 15.3
seconds, 0.60mph = 22.6 seconds;
ZB 0–50mph = 12.6 seconds,
0–60mph = 18.5 seconds
Number made: 12,754 (ZA), 23,846
(ZB)

1955–1959   MGA 1500
4 cylinder 73.025 × 88.9mm 1489cc
BHP: 68 at 5500rpm, later 72 at
5500rpm
4 forward speeds
Wheelbase: 94in
Max speed: 98mph
Acceleration: 0–50mph = 11 seconds,
0–60mph = 15.6 seconds, 0–70mph =
21.4 seconds, 0–80mph = 32.1 seconds
Number made: 58,750

1958–1960   MGA 'Twin Cam'
4 cylinder 75.414 × 88.9mm 1588cc
BHP: 108 at 6700rpm
4 forward speeds
Wheelbase: 94in
Top speed: 113mph
Acceleration: 0–50mph = 9.4 seconds,
0–60mph = 13.3 seconds, 0–70mph
17.3 seconds, 0–80mph = 22.5
seconds, 0–90mph = 30 seconds,
0–100mph = 41.1 seconds
NB: as tested by *The Autocar*; better
times have been recorded
Number made: 2111

**1959–1962   MGA 1600 (Mks I
and II)**
Mk I 4 cylinder 74.414 × 88.9mm
1588cc; Mk II 4 cylinder 76.2 ×
88.9mm 1622cc
BHP: Mk I 80 at 5600rpm, Mk II 93
at 5500rpm
4 forward speeds
Wheelbase: 94in
Max speed: 101mph
Acceleration: Mk I 0–50mph = 10.3
seconds, 0–60mph = 14.2 seconds,
0–70mph = 18.5 seconds, 0–80mph =
26.6 seconds, 0–90mph = 36.4 seconds
Mk II 0–50mph = 9.7 seconds,
0–60mph = 13.7 seconds, 0–70mph =
18.1 seconds, 0–80mph = 24.6
seconds, 0–90mph = 36.1 seconds
Number made: 31,501 (Mk I), 8719
(Mk II)

1959–1961   Magnette Mk III Saloon
4 cylinder 73.025 × 88.9mm 1489cc
BHP: 66 at 5200rpm
4 forward speeds
Wheelbase: 99¼in
Max speed: 85mph
Number made: 15,676

**1961–1964   Midget Mk I (GAN 1
and GAN 2)**
GAN 1 4 cylinder 62.9 × 76.2mm
948cc, GAN 2 4 cylinder 64.58 ×
83.72mm 1098cc
BHP: GAN 1 46 at 5500rpm, GAN 2
55 at 5500rpm
4 forward speeds
Wheelbase: 80in
Max speed: GAN 1 85mph, GAN 2
90mph
Acceleration: GAN 1 0–50mph = 14.4
seconds, 0–60mph = 20.2 seconds,
0–70mph = 32.8 seconds, 0–80mph =
56.8 seconds; GAN 2 0–50mph = 12
seconds, 0–60mph = 17.2 seconds,
0–70mph = 27.9 seconds, 0–80mph =
36.9 seconds
Number made: 16,080 (GAN 1),
9601 (GAN 2)

1961–1968   Magnette Mk IV Saloon
4 cylinder 76.2 × 88.9mm 1622cc
BHP: 68 at 5000rpm
4 forward speeds (automatic optional)
Wheelbase: 99¼in
Max speed: 85 + mph
Number made: 13,738

1962–1967   MGB Mk I
4 cylinder 80.26 × 88.9mm 1798cc
BHP: 95 at 5400rpm
4 forward speeds (overdrive optional)
Wheelbase: 91in
Max speed: 105mph
Acceleration: 0–50mph = 8.5 seconds,
0–60mph = 12.2 seconds, 0–70mph =
16.5 seconds, 0–80mph = 22.9
seconds, 0–90mph = 32.6 seconds,
0–100mph = 52.3 seconds
Number made: 137,733

**1962–1971   MG 1100/1300
Saloons Mk I and II**
1100 4 cylinder 64.58 × 83.72mm
1098 cc (1962–1967), 1300 4
cylinder 70.63 × 81.33mm 1275cc
(1967–1971)
BHP: 1100 55 at 5500rpm, 1300 70
at 6000rpm
4 forward speeds (automatic optional)
Wheelbase: 93½in
Max speed: 1100 80mph, 1300
90mph
Number made 116,827 (1100),
26,240 (1300)

1964–1966   Midget Mk II (GAN 3)
4 cylinder 64.58 × 83.72mm 1098cc
BHP: 59 at 5750rpm
4 forward speeds
Wheelbase: 80in
Max speed: 92mph
Acceleration: 0–50mph × 9.7 seconds,
0–60mph = 14.5 seconds, 9–70mph =
19.7 seconds, 0–80mph = 31.5
seconds
Number made- 26,601

**1966–1974   Midget Mk III (GAN 4
and GAN 5)**
4 cylinder 70.63 × 81.33mm 1275cc
BHP: 65 at 6000rpm
4 forward speeds
Wheelbase: 80in
Max speed: 94mph
Acceleration: 0–50mph = 9.6 seconds,
0–60mph W14.1 seconds, 0–70mph =
20 seconds, 0–80mph = 29.7 seconds
Number made: 13,722 (GAN 4),
86,650 (GAN 5)

1967–1969   MGC
6 cylinder 83.362 × 88.9mm 2912cc
BHP: 145 at 5250rpm
4 forward speeds (automatic optional)
Wheelbase: 91in
Max speed: 120mph
Acceleration: 0–50mph = 7.6 seconds,
0–60mph = 10 seconds, 0–70mph =
13.8 seconds, 0–80mph = 18 seconds,
0–90mph = 23.1 seconds, 0–100mph
= 29.3 seconds
Number made: 4542 (2 seat roadster),
4457 (GT coupe)

1967–1981   MGB Mk II
4 cylinder 80.26 × 88.9mm 1798cc
BHP: 95 at 5400rpm (not quoted
in USA)
4 forward speeds (automatic optional
1967–1973, overdrive standard from
1975 on)
Wheelbase: 91in
Max speed: 105mph
Acceleration: 0–50mph = 8.2 seconds,
0–60mph = 12.1 seconds, 0–70mph =
16.5 seconds, 0–80mph = 22.7
seconds, 0–90mph = 34.5 seconds
Number made: 375,000 (approx)

1972–1076   MGB GT V8
8 cylinder 88.9 × 71.12mm 3528cc
BHP: 137 at 5000rpm
4 forward speeds + overdrive
Wheelbase: 91in
Max speed: 124mph
Acceleration: 0–50mph = 6.4 seconds,
0–60mph = 8.6 seconds, 0–70mph =
11.8 seconds, 0–80mph = 15.1
seconds, 0–90mph = 19 seconds,
0–100mph = 25.3 seconds, 0–110mph
35.6 seconds
Number made: 2591

1974–1979   Midget Mk III (GAN 6)
4 cylinder 73.3 × 87.87.4mm 1491cc
BHP: 65 at 5500rpm
4 forward speeds
Wheelbase: 80in
Max speed: 101mph
Acceleration: 0–50mph = 8.5 seconds,
0–60mph = 12.3 seconds, 0–70mph =
17 seconds, 0–80mph = 24 seconds,
0–90mph = 35.3 seconds
Number made: 100,372

Index

Acknowledgments

The author and the publishers would like to thank Nick Georgano, Bridget Daly and Richard Nichols for their help in editing the book, David Eldred, who designed it, and Ronald Watson who compiled the index.

Special credit is due to Nicky Wright who took most of the photographs.

Thanks are due to the following who also supplied photographs:
Hilton Press Services: pages 7, 9, 10, 12, 13, 19, 20, 22, 23, 24, 25, 26, 27, 35, 46, 49, 51, 56, 57, 58, 70, 73, 77, 81, 92, 93, 96, 97, 98, 99, 104.

We would also like to thank the following owners who kindly allowed their superb automobiles to be photographed for this book:
Peter Agg (1932 MG F)
E D Alderson (1955 MG TF)
Paul Ahston (1934 MG PA)
Bud Basset (A-C-D Museum) (1962 MGA 1600)
Ian Davidson (1934 MG PA)
Peter Green (1934 MG Model ND)
Fred Hale (1936 MG SA)
Tim Hunt (1935 MG P 'Bongazoo')
George Jenkins (1936 MG PB)
Andrew Nairne (1950 MG TD)
Dixon Morris (1956 MG Magnette ZA)
Tony Roodhouse (1935 MG PB)
Dr Mark Sleep (1936 SA Tickford coupe)
John Thorley (MGB 45)
George A Ward (1933 MG KI Magnette)
Martin Warner (1935 MG KN Magnette)
David Washbourne (1936 MG SA)